To/
Colm, Miranda, Tiernan, Amelia

Best of luck on your American
Trip and you have a great
adventure and wonderful time

lots of love

Des & Estelle White.

DID I MENTION THE FREE WINE?

Madness, Mayhem & The Muse

On tour with Felix Dennis
by JASON KERSTEN

DID I MENTION THE FREE WINE?

Madness, Mayhem & The Muse

On tour with Felix Dennis
by JASON KERSTEN

Designed by Rebecca Jezzard · Illustrations by Paul Cox

1 3 5 7 9 10 8 6 4 2

Published in 2013 by Ebury Press, an imprint of Ebury Publishing

A Random House Group Company

Felix Dennis would like to thank the guest poets who performed on the 2010
'Did I Mention The Free Wine? Tour' for granting permission for their poems to be printed in this book.

The Random House Group Limited Reg. No. 954009

Addresses for companies within the Random House Group can be found at www.randomhouse.co.uk

A CIP catalogue record for this book is available from the British Library

The Random House Group Limited supports The Forest Stewardship Council® (FSC®), the leading international
forest certification organisation. Our books carrying the FSC label are printed on FSC® certified paper.
FSC is the only forest certification scheme endorsed by the leading environmental organisations, including Greenpeace.
Our paper procurement policy can be found at www.randomhouse.co.uk/environment

Illustrator: Paul Cox
Designer: Rebecca Jezzard
Production: Caroline Rush

Printed and bound by Butler Tanner & Dennis
Frome and London

Set in Sabon and Univers

ISBN 9780091951856

To buy books by your favourite authors and register for offers visit www.randomhouse.co.uk

To my daughter.

May she never wind up in the back
of a tour bus, unless it's her own.

GLASGOW

DID I MENTION THE FREE WINE?

DUBLIN

CORK

CARDIFF

EXETER

W

N

E

DID I MENTION THE FREE WINE TOUR 2010

Contents

Poems by Guest Poets

Poems by Felix Dennis

INTRODUCTION

There was once a time and place when only kings were more revered than the great travelling poets. A thousand years ago in ancient Ireland, bards not only crossed the land in processions of pomp and fanfare, but also were required by law to have a retinue of at least ten attendants. They were called poet-ollams – 'master poets' – and were versed in no fewer than 350 kinds of metre. No prince could refuse an ollam's visit or deny him or his servants full hospitality. Entire realms had to tighten their belts after these guests left, and a single poem composed and delivered on site could be worth a fortune. Bigger even than today's rock stars, they became a tribe so powerful in themselves that on three occasions they almost had to be banished from the land.

Felix Dennis would have loved those days. Given poetry's profit potential back then, there is no doubt in my mind that he would have been a poet-ollam, and he is the closest thing to a modern one we have. He has reversed the tradition only in the pragmatic sense that his fans are the ones who receive the gifts, but anyone who has ever attended his performances knows how special they are. His hospitality and presentation are unrivalled and he brings poetry back to where it belongs, with the people. And, believe me, he knows how to tour in style.

This book chronicles my experiences on tour with him through England, Wales, Ireland and Scotland in late 2010 – the most ambitious tour he had ever undertaken. He invited me along three weeks before he left. I had worked for him years earlier as a magazine editor and always wanted to know him better, but I also had a personal agenda. Sitting on my bookshelf was a small tin containing my share of my grandmother's ashes. She was one of my favourite people in all the world and had passed on six years earlier.

'I'll do it,' I told Felix in his New York City office as we negotiated the terms of my enlistment, 'provided that I can use your helicopter for the purposes of scattering my grandmother's ashes when we reach her home town, Edinburgh.'

His eyes rolled slowly into a long orbit behind those signature Theo Bifo bifocals of his. Helicopters are expensive, and he was already in the midst of a logistical maelstrom. My request meant more complications, half a dozen phone calls, legal uncertainty, possibly bribes. And yet, being Felix Dennis, he knew a sentimental trump card when he saw one.

'All right, done,' he finally said. We shook hands and looked each other in the eye to seal the deal.

I was so proud of myself. Here he was, an infamously sagacious negotiator worth almost half a billion pounds, and I, a writer of middling fame, had outmanoeuvred him. Even if he had said no to the chopper, I probably would have gone along and written about him anyway. A journalist can search his whole life and never find a specimen as fascinating as Felix Dennis. He was at a highly reflective period of his life – an unusual state for a man of constant action.

Of course, he may have outmanoeuvred *me*. It was still impossible to keep up with him and life on tour was gruelling. It took me two months to recover. The guy is a human singularity who generates his own laws of physics. Even in reflection he is on the prowl, and the only vessel capable of bottling his lightning is he. When it comes to studying a lone wolf, the best one can do is get a temporary bead on him before he moves out of range again and back into his solitude.

Felix Dennis performing live on stage

Photograph: Sebastian Rich 2011

place by getting as much out of writers as was humanly possible for as little as possible, it was time for lunch.

His residence, the Old Manor, is surprisingly small, like a hobbit hole. It's a delightfully cosy, thatched-roof home of three bedrooms, thoughtfully equipped but far from a palace. I had been in bigger, more ostentatious houses owned by men of far smaller means. Felix explained to me that most people only live in a few rooms they like; the rest is a waste.

'Watch your head there,' he warned, pointing out a low beam that dated back to the sixteenth century. 'It knocked out a journalist once.'

This was only the third time I had ever been alone with him. The second time, our meeting a few weeks earlier, had been brief and businesslike. The first had been in 2003, after the Dennis Publishing Poetry Contest. He was fresh into his new life as a poet and had challenged his employees in the USA to write poems about working for his company. The winner was promised a meal with Felix. So I spent about three hours working up a little testimony about life as a *Maxim* editor. I wanted to win. I wanted to know better the man I worked for, and tell him why I felt the magazine was becoming a parody of itself, no longer taking the creative risks that made it great or true to its core conception. (This happens to all successful magazines. They can be reborn and refreshed and go on to new heights, but the formative spark can never be re-created. I was very young and naïve.) In a company of three hundred, I felt that what I was doing was my best chance of getting an audience with the king. And I won.

Three months later, I was summoned to a conference room and sat down at a table piled with sandwiches and fine French wine. We were alone for about five minutes, until both the president and the publisher sat down too. This was not what I had envisioned, which was a dinner at Keen's Steak House followed by cigarettes and cognac in the smoking room. In spite of that, I still told Felix what I thought, and he agreed with me wholeheartedly – so much so that he summoned the entire staff of *Maxim* into the conference room to give us all a pep talk. As they walked in, they looked at me as if I had caused them to walk on burning coals. My big one-on-one with Felix had turned into a staff meeting. It took me weeks of apologies to recover their faith. In any other company, someone would have come up with an excuse to fire me three weeks later.

So here we were, finally, brought together again by poetry. The last time I had heard any news of him was two years earlier when, in a drunken fugue, he had sworn to a reporter from the *Times* that he had murdered a man by pushing him off a cliff. His victim was an abuser of a woman and child and they were an episode away from being killed themselves. The next day he had denied everything, dismissing it as a drunken fantasy, but the story had wildfired across the Internet. I had to get that elephant out of the way, especially since we were drinking ourselves.

'So are you gonna tell me who you killed?'

'I'll have to kill *you* if I do.'

'That's not a denial.'

We spent the rest of the afternoon drinking more and discussing Roman and medieval history, politics, his dogs and his house. Later on, a friend and neighbour of his, Igor Kolodotschko, joined us in the conservatory – a buoyant, glass-enclosed room where Felix often composes poetry and hangs out. Igor regaled me with stories about a road trip he'd taken through the States forty years earlier. He was a millionaire himself, though, as with Felix, you'd never know it. That afternoon was everything I had wanted years earlier; I was getting to know my old boss. As the golden glow of Chablis went into overdrive, I suddenly heard the distant, rapidly increasing drone of a helicopter.

'You'll want to see this,' Felix said.

Moments later, a white, piscine-looking helicopter hovered gently downward into a cow pasture across the road. It was remarkably quiet. 'That's the fastest civilian helicopter in the world,' Felix added.

Pleasantly buzzed on two fronts, we crossed the road and climbed in. As the whirlybird rose, several of his ground staff waved goodbye from the edge of a wooden fence. Seconds later, we were cruising over the green puzzle board of central England at 1500 feet and 220 knots. The world's first and only helicopter poet was going on tour.

This was Felix's fifth poetry tour in eight years. *Tales From The Woods* was his sixth book of poems; no small feat for a man who hadn't begun writing until his fifties. Back when he started, plenty of folks, myself included, had been convinced that it was a doomed enterprise, that it wouldn't last, that he would move on to new diversions. Yet even now, long after he had thrown his hat in to the ring, his obsession was not only unabated but increasing. We would cover over 2811 miles on the tour – just about the length of Chile – but it was really only a small fraction of a longer journey that had begun on 13 September 1999.

Like so many of his stories, the one about how he became a poet had a fateful, apocryphal ring. He was in a London hospital, recovering from a hypothyroid condition which was in turn related to his years of narcotic abuse, when the muse struck. She attacked at the precise moment when he was at his weakest and most vulnerable: sitting on the edge of his bed, wearing only a pink nylon gown in the cold, institutional air. Suddenly, the words of Dorothy Parker's poem, 'Resume' came into his mind…

> Razors pain you;
> Rivers are damp;
> Acids stain you;
> And drugs cause cramp.
> Guns aren't lawful;
> Nooses give;
> Gas smells awful;
> You might as well live.

Publishing's in-house marketing and design department, usually occupied with hawking mass-market magazines, was tasked with promotion. They designed posters, flyers, advertisements, programmes, cards – all for the boss's personal poetry enterprise. It was the job of Jerina Hardy, Felix's young PR specialist, to woo local and national media and convince them that their shows, programmes and publications would not be complete without interviews and profiles of The Man. With a staff of four, she contacted every outfit in Ireland and the UK short of ham radio operators. She also needed to make sure that every event was known about in its locality, which meant contacting all universities, poetry societies, galleries, museums, cafés and key venues asking them to display posters and flyers about the tour. Press material, posters and flyers then had to be mailed to every one of them. A month before the show, another team was employed to visit the cities and pepper them with flyers. As if all of this weren't ambitious enough, Felix decided to sell the tickets online. His IT specialist, Jonathan Noone, designed and programmed a computer system that not only sold tickets four different ways but also generated daily sales reports.

I had seen only the tail end of all these preparations when I arrived in London a week earlier, but it struck me as bizarre in the extreme: one of the world's highest and most revered art forms married to a highly systematic and sagaciously capitalistic attempt to make it and its practitioner as accessible as possible to the public. His offices in Kingly Street on the edge of Soho resembled nothing so much as a political headquarters. Downstairs was a 'war room' with a whiteboard and the names of all the cities, along with those of the guest poets he had invited to perform each night and the number of tickets that had been sold at each. To an American it was reminiscent of a congressional strategy board for the gaining of votes. Brighton: sold out. Cork: 29 tickets left. Dublin: 200 left. Calling in from his country home the poet demanded daily updates from Jonathan.

Hundreds of empty seats in Dublin? Where were the Irish? Surely the land that had produced Yeats, Wilde and Heaney should have a better turnout. Eighty seats left in London? Fifty in Birmingham? Not good enough. Call the universities! Sell 'em at half price! Slowly but surely, the words 'SOLD OUT' began appearing next to the cities names on the whiteboard. Had Felix been a US politician, a similar effort would have easily been enough to get him elected to a small congressional district, possibly even the governorship of Alaska.

The cost of the tour alone was probably more than all the world's poets had made in the last year. Wine and catering ran to nearly £100,000, the helicopter cost £50,000, and stage production over £100,000. Then there were printing and promotion, venue hire, merchandising, advertising, filming, staff expenses, ticket booking, public relations, web marketing, mobile phone costs and the inevitable unforeseen. In all, it came to nearly half a million pounds. Even flesh and bone could become a line item. On the Friday before the tour launch Felix's Group Finance Director, Ian Leggett, bounded into the war room seeking answers from anyone to a question that had been nagging him for days.

'Would you pay £9000 to insure something worth £400,000?' he asked.

'That depends,' I replied. 'What do you want to insure?'

'Felix.'

This was distressing news. Putting a price on a human being is cynical enough, but I had thought that Felix was worth at least £500 million. Had the Great Recession hit him *that* hard? Was he hocked down to his last few hundred thousand quid or, even worse, smoking crack again? Most importantly, would I be paid?

'Felix has to be worth more than that.'

'For the tour, you ninny, the *tour*,' Ian said. 'You know, if something happens to him and the show can't go on, we've gotta cover the costs.'

Now that made sense. His private office had invested a wheelbarrow of money, and all of it was riding on the immediate fate of a guy who had stood on death's doorstep three times, and would probably have pneumonia by Tuesday. Then there are always accidents. Death by tour is a real risk, especially for the jet and chopper set, although Felix had gone to impressive lengths to ensure he didn't pull a Buddy Holly. He had hired a helicopter that had not only two engines, but two pilots, just in case one of these thirty-year-olds happened to die of a heart attack during the hour or two it took to fly anywhere in England. More remotely, there was also the 'grudge and a gun' scenario. Surely a man as rich as Felix had asylums full of enemies. What better chance to off him than when he's on stage, à la Jenny Fields in *The World According to Garp*? I could see him toppling away from the podium, mortally wounded. What would his last words be? Knowing him, they would almost certainly be a piece of invective directed at his assassin.

'Well?' said Ian impatiently.

'If you had a £400,000 car, you'd insure it for £9000' wouldn't you?' a young intern named Rebecca Ridge finally asked in return.

'That is a really good way of looking at it,' said Ian, and tromped back upstairs to ring Lloyd's of London.

Never go back

[To D.G.L.S. who has lived by this creed.]

Never go back. Never go back.
Never return to the haunts of your youth.
Keep to the track, to the beaten track,
Memory holds all you need of the truth.

Never look back. Never look back.
Never succumb to the gorgon's stare.
Keep to the track, to the beaten track,
No-one is waiting and nothing is there.

Never go back. Never go back.
Never surrender the future you've earned.
Keep to the track, to the beaten track,
Never return to the bridges you burned.

Never look back. Never look back.
Never retreat to the 'glorious past'.
Keep to the track, to the beaten track,
Treat every day of your life as your last.

Never go back. Never go back.
Never acknowledge the ghost on the stair.
Keep to the track, to the beaten track,
No-one is waiting and nothing is there.

But that wasn't the Felix Dennis way. After Felix's 'factotum' Toby Fisher, wearing a white 'Did I Mention The Free Wine 2010 Tour' t-shirt, had introduced him, Felix – costumed in his trademark bifocals, a cream dress shirt and an orange waistcoat – strutted on to the stage and took up position behind a lectern disguised as a tree trunk. There were projection screens on either side of him, and covering the stage was a giant rug stitched with the same 'Green Man' portrait by Bill Sanderson that graced the jacket of *Tales From The Woods*.

He had announcements to make prior to reciting. After all, he had sponsors. In addition to his partners at The Week Wines and The Week Travel Agency, he thanked HSBC bank: 'Just this one time, thanks to the bank.' It was surreal, but if there was one thing that I would learn about Felix Dennis over the next month, it was that not trying to make money was impossible for him. He obviously hadn't become a poet for profit, but he'd be damned if he didn't try to make it pay. His final announcement: no one would be hearing free verse tonight. He was firmly encamped with Robert Frost, who had once said of writing free verse, 'I'd just as soon play tennis with the net down.'

And then the show began. Felix's voice, chiselled by a lifetime of cigarettes and controlled substances, was deep and expressive. He didn't recite his poems but performed them, lingering on syllables, pausing for effect, belting out tempo, even shouting. Surprise, anger, exhaustion, contempt, chagrin, emptiness, morosity, fear, mockery, indignity, love, hatred, nostalgia – he conveyed all these emotions and probably more, in tones that were sometimes sardonic, at others irritated, paternal, or celebratory. Every line, every word was projected and accentuated for maximum effect. He used his body as an instrument, pacing the stage, hunching over, throwing out his arms and kicking up his legs. He made eye contact with his audience. For the more serious poems he retreated behind the tree trunk, but most of the time he was on the prowl, commanding attention and reaction.

All the while, images danced on the screens. Sometimes they were short films and animations with themes appropriate to the poem; at other times it was a live close-up of Felix. At all times the words to each poem were projected up there for the audience to follow. There was multi-coloured mood lighting and occasionally even background music. His introductions to his poems were polished, entertaining and mercifully concise. And he wasn't going to let his audience have all the fun; he had two glasses of wine up there to start, one red, one white. Now and then, he'd call on Toby for a refill.

However much his critics sneered and derided him as an amateur, I had a hard time believing that there wasn't something they could learn from him. He was unquestionably engaging, and he worked his ass off up there to connect. Before seeing him that night, my biggest worry had been that he wouldn't be good, that I had signed up for an awkward vanity excursion. That fear was eliminated by his third poem, when I realised that this was the most entertaining poetry reading I had ever attended. At several points I turned and stared at my fellow audience members, and not a single eye wandered. They were transfixed, smiling, soaking it in. Between poems they'd drink their wine, but often they forgot to do so because they were too busy watching him.

'He was absolutely fantastic,' an American woman on holiday told me during the interval. 'I've seen him three times now. He just gets better and better.' If there were any disappointed customers in Exeter, they had left early. All I heard for the rest of the night was the sound of pouring wine and good cheer.

His top-notch performance was also witnessed by one of the UK's finest comediennes, Dawn French, who later came backstage to congratulate Felix on a spectacular show.

After the show, people lined up thirty deep to buy from the merchandise mound and have Felix sign their books. It took him an hour to work through the crowd. When he was finished, he hopped back into the Range Rover with Toby and headed for his helicopter like a rock star. But there would be no returning to a mansion for me. I was issued a blanket and pillow, and shown to a sailor's bunk on a bus crammed with nine other roadies. I was now part of the tour, a member of the entourage, a fly in the wine.

The tour bus had looked impressive in photos that Felix had posted on Facebook a few weeks earlier. A navy blue double-decker, it had a conference table that seated six, two flat screen TVs with DVD players, onboard internet, plus a galley whose contents included a fridge and microwave. All that, and it could sleep thirteen, including the driver. 'We're gonna roll like rock stars,' I'd thought to myself as I gazed at the snapshots. My friends were jealous.

Never trust a photograph from a guy who's made millions doctoring up two-dimensional images. Stepping aboard in Exeter, I immediately knew that living aboard this machine with nine other people would constitute the greatest challenge of the tour.

It only looked like a double-decker from the outside. With the exception of the galley, it was just the top deck that housed passengers. The rest, which I had foolishly assumed would contain a jacuzzi and a shower and a trampoline, was for storing stage equipment and the formidable stacks of Felix Dennis paraphernalia. At best, the conference table sat no more than two comfortably. One of the TVs was broken, and the galley was strategically located right at the entrance, so that whenever you left the door open for fresh air the punters could stick their head in and beg you for a glass of wine, which occurred on several occasions. There was no shower. Worst of all, for some strange reason that no one could explain at the time, we were only allowed to use the loo for Number One. I would later learn that this is true of almost all live-aboard buses. Although there is theoretically nothing preventing Number Two, the resultant smell has a way of invading the bus afterwards and turning it into a rolling outhouse.

At least I'll have my own bunk, I thought to myself, and set off for the sleeping area. In Felix's photos, this appeared as a long, sumptuous hall filled with compartments so spacious that you could rent them out to the citizens of space-starved Tokyo. Tastefully carpeted in plush red and grey, with green LED lights running along it, it had a *Starship Enterprise* kind of feel. But when I attempted to make my way down this hallway, it brought to mind quite another type of vessel.

Das Boot is the only World War II film in which you can guiltlessly root for the Germans because the conditions aboard the U-boat are so cramped and abominable that even the Nazis deserve victory just for being there. Dishes falling from their compartments, greasy bodies contorting for space to pass each other, fighting not to piss on your own two feet as you stood in the miniscule loo – the only things *Das Boot* had that this one didn't were torpedoes and a periscope. Later, I would become half convinced that the bus was a conscious, demonic entity bent on exacting as much discomfort from its passengers as possible.

I could go on, and I will later. Suffice it to say, when I threw my bags into my lower bunk (tops were all taken) an imaginary letter home began forming in my mind: *Dear Mum, I've joined the Royal Navy…*

Then I ran off to meet my shipmates.

The female, and vastly superior, portion of our crew consisted of four women. Chief among these was Wendy Kasabian, who was one of Felix's two personal assistant and had worked for him on and off for thirty-four years. She had curly brown hair and a ready smile and looked far too young to have crewed that long on Felix's mad ship of fools, and had an inherently optimistic demeanour that no doubt helped enable her to weather it all. She had spent her teenage years in America, had more patience than your mother, and if you crossed her she was like a voodoo witch: she had ways of making you pay without you or even Felix ever knowing it.

Caroline Rush, Felix's other PA and the woman who had scouted the tour, was from Stratford-upon-Avon, not far from Felix's country home, and in temperament reminded me very much of what people have told me about myself. She was a pleasant, easy-going person to be around, and if she was particularly happy or pissed off you knew it because she'd tell it to your face. Caroline and I also liked the same kinds of food, and sometimes I wondered if that contributed to our shared temperaments. She had straight brown hair, green eyes, and the ability to get tremendous amounts of work done without making it look like work.

The youngest of our girls was Jerina Hardy, Felix's publicist, which has to be one of the most difficult jobs on the planet. We are, after all, talking about someone tasked with putting a good face on the first human ever to utter the word 'cunt' on British television. Jerina was by far the most conscientious, earnest, healthy, and under-appreciated of us all. Later on, she would lament the fact that I never wrote about her in my blog; that was because she was the only well-adjusted person among us and therefore deserved protecting.

Last but not least among the women was Marie-France, the longtime companion of Felix's heart. She had been with him for almost twenty-five years, and although she had the option of flying back home with him every night on the helicopter she had chosen to be on the bus.

'The bus is where the party is,' she explained to me that first night. 'The helicopter is so boring.'

I have a great ear when it comes to pronouncing accents, but a terrible one for writing them, so I follow the advice of one of my old teachers and don't even try. Let's just say that the way Marie-France says 'boring' penetrates the air with so much Gallic contempt that you hope to hell she never uses it to describe you. Hearing that, there was but one first impression to be had: this woman was literally down to earth. In all those years with Felix she had never given an interview to the press, so I would make it my mission to see if I could get her to open up.

The girls, I realised that first night, had touring all figured out. They had brought twice as much luggage as any of us men, and consequentially commandeered an entire section above the driver that would otherwise be used as a work station with a nice view. They had made sure they occupied the four bunks closest to it, so that it essentially became their closet. When we all prepared to bed down that night they hung a sheet in front of their section, then emerged from behind it wearing matching plaid pyjamas that Wendy had bought to unite the sisterhood.

With the exception of Jonathan Noone and myself, all the male passengers on the bus worked for Class Act, the event production company that handled the show's technical details. This formidable outfit was headed up by Mick Watson. As the man in the bunk above me, he would become my personal alarm clock. Mick's right-hand man, and a partner since the beginning, was Thom Stretton, a jolly, six-foot-three bloke from Buckinghamshire with a Lemmy moustache. Ex-British Army, Thom was more comfortable with the living conditions than any of us; during the shows he was charged with managing overall sound and the audio-visual presentation on the twin screens behind Felix. Jamie Broome, who ran the in-house camera, was the quietest of us all, but when he did speak he had the diction and precision of an old-school stage actor. Class Act was also a family operation, with Mick's two sons, Scott and Tom, working sound, lighting and subtitles.

Tom Rooke and Jerina's little brother, Jack, were not on the bus, but they might as well have been; they zipped ahead of us in a hire car, staying in hotels after packing up Felix's books and merchandise into the luggage compartments. Both of them were good-spirited, energetic recent college graduates out for adventure and some spending dough.

I'd get to know all of them better over the course of the next six weeks; some more, some less. To a certain degree, all of them were initially suspicious of my purpose. Felix, after all, had shot me into their midst like a free radical. 'Oh yes, by the way, a writer will be on board,' he'd notified them, 'but don't worry, he's under my control.'

Famous last words.

All Nature's Art

All Nature's Art is purest accident,
Not in or of itself—how should she know?—
But in the quality of what is lent
By those who view what Providence made so.

Take grass of softest green— in beetles' eyes
A dreary, harsh savanna, spiked and bound
In monochrome and perilous disguise:
To us a lawn— to hens, a killing ground.

And so it is, my love, with you and me—
This old fool's eyes were ever drawn to youth;
Though Nature's Art lies not in what we see,
Such 'seeing' smooths the wilderness of truth.

Though as for that, no truth was ever known
To topple skin-deep Beauty from her throne.

An Old Dog Is The Best Dog

An old dog is the best dog,
A dog with rheumy eyes;
An old dog is the best dog
A dog grown sad and wise;
    Not one who snaps at bubbles,
        Nor one who barks at nowt —
            A dog who knows your troubles,
                A dog to see you out.

An old bitch is the best bitch,
Not pups to fetch your sticks;
An old bitch is the best bitch,
Not one to teach new tricks;
    Not one who's up and leaping,
        But one whose coat is grey —
            Leg's twitching while she's sleeping
                In dreams of yesterday.

of the bourgeoisie, he was indisputably a free-thinker and a contrarian himself. Therefore he should be spared when the revolution finally came, although his wealth would still have to be redistributed. Plus, providing free wine and canapés to the proletariat was not something to be forgotten.

Through no fault of Class Act's, the sound was abominable that night. The Northumberland's ballroom was intended for weddings, not poets, and Felix sounded like he was playing in a Tube station. In spite of that, the audience was buzzing with delight. During the interval, I checked back with the first group. They were all smiling happily except Ms Barry. One of Felix's poems had brought tears to her eyes.

'I couldn't believe it – he made me cry!' she said.

These were tears of sentiment, positive emotions that he had drawn out of her with his poetry. Being able to do that is the closest one can get to casting a real magic spell. After the show, I rushed back to the green room to tell Felix the news.

'She cried, eh?' he shrugged. 'Good.'

Everything went downhill after that. One of the Irish communists spilled wine on a well-dressed businessman sitting next to him. Verbal assaults ensued, and the revolution could have started right there if Wendy hadn't intervened and offered to pay for dry cleaning.

'Who's going to pay for it? You?' said the offended man.

'Even Felix Dennis gets his suits cleaned,' she said archly, then wrote down his name. She took it from all sides that night, especially me.

'When are we eating?' I asked her a few minutes after Felix left. It was 11p.m. and my stomach was rumbling.

'You'll have to fend for yourself tonight,' she said. On an empty stomach, it is a fact that I can become a complete, self-obsessed bastard. Suddenly I had a horrible vision: collecting receipts for the next month, sorting through a rat's nest of paper, and finally battling Felix's accounting department over dozens of coffees and cheap lunches consumed in British cities I couldn't even remember.

'That's not in my contract,' I told Wendy. 'I don't pay for my meals.' Forget the fact that I was supposed to be part of a team, or that it would probably be just three or four receipts, not fifty, and that I had no reason to believe that anybody was out to screw me: it was just an obnoxious thing to say. And I said it several more times, until Wendy was marching a bunch of us out the door to round up some McDonald's. She was fuming, and it was only when we were about halfway to McD's that I realised nobody had eaten. My failing that night was being a shit to the one person who always took more of it than anybody and deserved it the least. Once I'd understood that she would feed me, I apologised to her profusely and asked her to forgive me, like the pathetic child I was.

'I'll think about it,' she said.

and an MTV video.

'Why do they call you "Danger"?' I asked him early in the tour. He fired up his laptop and showed me some videos taken many years earlier. In one, he was attempting to jump into his drum set. He ended up toppling off the stage and injuring himself; in the other, he was street surfing on the back of his motorcycle, hands free.

So he was our driver.

In point of fact, he was a magnificent driver. In addition to motoring seamlessly through psychotic episode-inducing London traffic, he could back that bus and trailer down cobbled streets you'd think were too narrow to piss in. On the job, he was completely unflappable – precisely the kind of person you want with your life in his hands.

The rest of us lay in our bunks at night and dreamed of home; to Steve the bus <u>was</u> his home. He slept in a tiny crypt-like arrangement carved out of the stairs just behind the front passenger seat. It had no windows, and its entrance was smaller than that of a beaver lodge. The first time I had to bother him, I couldn't even find his lair. I went up front, shouted his name, and was about to leave when suddenly I saw his bald, talking head poking out of a hole in the wall like a demented game trophy.

'What is it, mate?' he said, bleary-eyed.

'Sorry to wake you….You sleep in there, huh?'

'Sleep. Live. Wank. Everything but shag, mate. Not much room for that. Not that I haven't tried.'

'I, uh…How the hell do you get in there?'

'Well, it's not easy. I get on me hands and knees, then slowly straighten out me legs and back in. It's the only way.'

'I'd think head first would be easier.'

'It's the natural inclination, but you can't do that. One time, when I was a bit drunk and tired, I did go in head first. I'll never do that again. You can't turn around in there – it's a trap. Go in head first and you won't get out.'

'Jesus. So how *did* you get out?'

'Yelled and yelled, and finally some passengers came and pulled me out by me feet. Took about ten minutes.'

Despite the fact that I had woken him up, and was now bothering him with stupid questions, he was perfectly civil. How he managed to stay so calm while driving busloads of musicians and tourists around trafficky cities beat me. At first I thought he had to be on drugs himself, but then of course he couldn't be because he'd be tested. Eventually I concluded that the little trap door was a portal to another dimension. While we lay like mummies in our bunks, he was teleported across space and time, home to his girlfriend, or roaming through fields of wildflowers and rainbows and naked women on another planet. It was a devil's bargain that he had made with the bus in exchange for keeping it supplied with fresh souls to feed on.

is to speak with their spirit alone. I sensed that he had come outside to do just that, but had run into me.

No sooner had I stepped into the theatre's crowded foyer than I again ran into Lisa, who looked upset.

'There's a very angry guy here who wants to have it out with Felix,' she told me. 'He says Felix owes him money for some Frank Zappa photos. He's very creepy and I'm worried he'll do something.'

'Where is he?'

'I can't see him. He must have gone back into the theatre. He was older – about Felix's age.'

Great. Some hippie, probably from the Oz days, was stalking Felix at his own poetry gig. So much for peace and love where money is concerned. Under normal circumstances, watching two aging hippies fight it out would have been highly entertaining, but with Felix mourning Pat Leaver this obviously wasn't the night. He was liable to kill the guy. Yet before Lisa and I could get a bead on the grudge-bearer, the interval was over.

I couldn't imagine how Felix felt, having to perform in front of 215 people right after learning that a dear friend of forty years had died, but he held it together like a pro. Rather than setting his grief aside for the evening, he addressed it, dedicating a recital of 'I Just Stepped Out' to Pat. He would do this every night for the rest of the tour.

I stayed close to him at the book signing, thinking that Zappa Man might try to get in the queue and cause trouble when it was his turn, but he never showed up. Perhaps, after hearing the second set, he too realised that demanding money from Felix that night was off limits.

8 Bath

Komedia · 265 in attendance · 243 bottles consumed · guest poet Alison Brackenbury

Felix is the only poet I've ever heard of who expects his audience to behave like headbangers at a metal concert. He can be reciting in front of a packed house full of people thoroughly enjoying themselves, but unless he hears shouts, whistles and whoops he'll trudge into the dressing room at the interval looking like he's just swallowed some sour milk.

'What's wrong with these people?' he'll say. 'They're floating in formaldehyde out there! What do they want?'

Such inflated expectations no doubt come from his days as a rhythm & blues musician. By the time he was fifteen, he had moved away from home and into what he would later write about in his poem 'A Room of My Own'. In what must have been one of his earliest business ventures, he rented it out to friends for liaisons with girls while he was playing in a blues band.

Luckily, he had no complaints at Bath's Komedia, which hosted his most lively crowd yet. After he'd delivered some particularly rousing renditions of 'A Room of My Own' and 'Anti-Social Behaviour Orders' during the first set, the audience cheered and hollered. He came backstage positively pumped.

'That's more like it. Best night yet,' he declared as he stepped outside for a smoke. He had had somewhat lesser expectations from this posh town.

'I guess you can't judge a book by its cover,' I remarked. Well, that got him going. He started singing Bo Diddly's 'You Can't Judge a Book by Its Cover.'

You can't judge an apple by looking at a tree

You can't judge honey by looking at the bee

You can't judge a daughter by looking at the mother

You can't judge a book by looking at the cover

His voice was impassioned and husky and pleasant enough. I've heard him croon out some lovely Stones' tunes, including a particularly melodious 'As Tears Go By'. But Bo Diddly? There was just too much of the Thames in his voice and not enough Mississippi mud. But it was fun to see him enjoying himself so much.

Just then a stunning young blonde in a blue-green dress walked up with a tall fellow in a pink sports jacket. The British male's propensity for pink is one of those cultural peculiarities that has always puzzled me, along with painting targets on their planes. In and of itself, pink is lovely, but I've noticed that a lot of guys in the financial industry wear it. Maybe they want us to think that's how their balance sheets read. But it's a slippery slope. If he gets too comfortable, he'll soon be wearing a scarf daintily thrown back and mink gloves that he just can't get dirty. When your closet gets that full, it's time to step out of it.

The man introduced himself, but I only heard his last name: 'Rothschild'. His date had just flown in from Kiev. She was pure Slavic beauty, with impeccable skin and startling green eyes. As often happens with Felix, the male visitor wanted to talk about money. He and his friend had just read How to Get Rich, and 'found it great fun, if it weren't for the fact that we are millionaires.'

'It's not to be taken too serious,' Felix said. 'If you follow the book, it will screw up your life.'

'It screws up my life,' the man said, letting Felix know, once again, that he was part of the club. At that, the challenge was on.

'Yes, well, if you really want to be rich, it's very difficult to have proper relationships,' Felix said.

'I don't know. I find it liberating.'

'Yes, but if it came down to seeing your darling, or making £50,000 that night, which one would it be?'

'I would see my darling.'

'Then you ain't gonna get rich. Ha ha ha ha!'

'What is "rich", in your book?'

'Yeah, well, that's everybody,' Felix sighed. 'You could say that someone who has almost no money at all but doesn't want any is rich as Croesus.'

'Would you spend time or the £50,000?'

'Well, I've already made my choice. That's why I don't have anybody lovely like this.'

'You can come to Ukraine,' the young woman said coyly.

'You misunderstand me. I've been to bed with many of the most beautiful women in the world, but that's got nothing to do with anything. That's got everything to do with dollars. And it was great fun, I'm not pretending any different. Anyone who's had a lost decade that lasts for fifteen years is not that bad off. But in the end you have to make a choice, and I probably made the wrong one.'

After a bit of small talk, it was almost time for Felix to perform again. We stepped back inside the theatre doorway where he shook his head, visibly irritated.

'I think he's an exploiter,' he said. 'He's not a millionaire, and I don't think his name is Rothschild.'

'How do you know that?'

'I can spot 'em a mile away. I never, never miss.'

It took a moment for me to register what was going down. Why would Felix care so much whether this guy was a millionaire scion or a pretender? But the answer came as fast as the question: he cared because he had grown up bent on rising above his class in a society where class is often ruthlessly enforced, and he'd taken no short cuts himself. It went back to the expensive watch. Sizing people up based on appearance was second nature to him, and pretenders were his least favourite animal. They didn't play fair and were to be exposed. Much later in the tour I'd learn that I was no less exempt from his scrutiny and snap competitive judgement.

I was inclined to agree about the Rothschild guy. We'd had dozens of fans approach Felix. No doubt many were millionaires themselves, but this guy was the only one trying really hard to show it. Whatever the truth, it was clear that Felix was out to impress the young Ukrainian fox. He began his second set by remarking to the audience that there was an 'absolutely stunning' young woman in the audience, and he wanted to prove to her that he had once been an R&B musician. He then got the audience to stamp their feet in rhythm and belted out more Bo Diddly. That got them shouting even louder.

As he signed books afterwards Wendy Kasabian ran up to me. 'See that woman over there?' she said, pointing to a comely middle-aged lady decked out in a rhinestone jacket. 'Two years ago, she asked Felix to autograph her breasts.'

'I don't believe you.'

'Go and ask her.'

So I did. After a brief flash of embarrassment, the woman rolled her eyes, remembering the moment, and replied, 'I couldn't help it. I was so turned on.'

I embarrassed myself in Bath. After the show, most of the crew had a lovely dinner at a lively seafood restaurant. It was the first truly good meal of the tour, and since we had the next day off the order of the day was to put one on. After many drinks and good fun, I brought up something that had been bothering me since the beginning of the tour. We were supposed to be tour monkeys, rock 'n' rollers, hard partying, creative types – wasn't this the whole point of the bus? Clearly, it was all too tame. We were the lamest group of roadies Captain Danger had ever seen. No one had slept with anybody. Nobody had exposed themselves or been arrested. We were working for a guy who had spent much of his life worshipping drugs, sex and rock 'n' roll and we were on tour. Other than a few Valium pills to get to sleep, the only drug we had consumed was the last legal one.

'We need some weed on the bus!' I declared at the table. 'How come nobody has any weed?'

Looks were exchanged all around. Oh boy, we've spent all day wrangling shit for Felix. Now the Yank wants some weed.

'Look, I barely ever smoke it myself,' I continued, 'but it's only proper. This is a tour. A little Mary on the bus is okay. We have principles to uphold. Doesn't anybody here smoke out once in a while? What's happened to this country?'

Nobody had any. This was touring in the twenty-first century, where everybody was worried about their corporate job.

Nobody knew where to get any, but fool that I was, I wouldn't let it go. 'It's a city, right? Don't any of you know people here? Jesus, it shouldn't be that hard. There's always a place.'

To my surprise, one of my comrades whipped out a mobile and made a couple of calls. Intelligence of a certain nearby square where illicit dealings took place was returned to us, but then I realised that buying weed on street corners in a strange town wasn't exactly the best move for me either. Faced with the prospect of scoring for myself in a strange place, the decision was easy, even in my inebriated state. I went back to our rented flat (a night's respite from the bus) Skyped my wife, then slept until noon the next day.

'Don't be too embarrassed,' Danger told me later. 'It's almost the same in the music industry now. Nobody knows how to do it right anymore. Everybody's too afraid – even the young people are all about the money. The rock 'n' roll lifestyle isn't exactly dead, but it's definitely endangered.'

A Room of My Own

(My first bedsit — St. Kildas Road, Harrow-on-the-Hill)

A bed by the window — a double an' all!
A sink in the corner, the lav' down the hall,
Linoleum nailed to the planks on the floor,
And to top it all off, a lock on the door!

A view of a garden where nothing will grow,
Gas in the meter a shilling a throw,
Wallpaper roses whose petals have blown,
A table, a chair and a room of my own.

The table-top clouded with gouges and glue,
No witch in the wardrobe, a hanger or two,
I open my suitcase and fill up a drawer
While my eyes caress the lock on the door.

A room of my own! I shall put up a shelf
And fill it with books I've chosen myself,
And prune all the landlady's roses away
With posters of Lennon and Jimmy and Ché.

I'll paint all the light bulbs a luminous red,
And Jane will come over and leap in the bed,
And we'll smoke & make love & giggle & plan
As Bob whines 'Hey! Mr. Tambourine Man...'

* * *

And now I've a mansion with locks by the score,
But nobody leaps in my bed anymore,
It's forty years on, and the roses have blown —
And a man could get lost in a room of his own.

CHAPTER TEN
LIVERPOOL

The Contemporary
Urban Centre

220

118

Stephen Devereux

10 Liverpool

The Contemporary Urban Centre · 220 in attendance · 118 bottles consumed · guest poet Stephen Devereux

We woke up in a coach park south of the Albert Docks, near the new convention centre. Surrounding us was a concrete hinterland that felt so far from the city centre that we debated calling a cab. The day was bright, but my internal forecast was much darker.

Since the beginning of the tour, there had been a persistent hacking cough inside the bus. It was always there in the background, but you heard it most in the mornings, as we lay awake in our bunks on our backs – a scratchy, intermittent chorus of lung song. Eventually we decided that it was a Caribbean stowaway: MF had contracted it in Mustique, then brought it aboard the bus. The close, dank quarters, combined with occupants who ate poorly and drank excessively, created the perfect conditions for the infection to spread – a Petri dish on wheels. From MF, The Cough, as we came to call it, had moved to Caroline and then Wendy and Jerina and Jonathan, working its way down the bunks like the US Marines through the South Pacific in World War II. Once it got you, you had it for the duration. And by the end of the tour no one had escaped it.

'Keep that shit away from me,' Felix had told me a few days earlier when I mentioned that plague had arrived. Still recovering from his own infection, the mere hint of a pulmonary chortle could cause him to avoid you for an entire evening.

'Who gave you The Cough when you were in Mustique?' I had asked MF one night.

'Who do you think? Who was the first one you heard coughing?'

So that confirmed it. Felix was afraid of catching his own cough.

I had felt the first throaty itch the night before, and foolishly tried to salve it with free wine. I'd made it to sleep okay, but there was now no doubt. I had become one of the infected.

'Lemsip,' Wendy declared down in the galley. She opened up a tin box of pills, lozenges and powders. I'd never heard of any of them because they were all British, which gave me hope: maybe they were better than the over-the-counter crap we take in America in the hope that we won't have to hit the antibiotics later. Lemsip turned out to be the same chalky yellow sand, but it got me out of the door. Not that I lasted long. All I had energy for that day was a group lunch, then it was back to the bus to convalesce. Liverpool looked like an interesting place, but the Maritime Museum was closed and I wasn't going to miss seeing the next three cities by pushing my failing health to visit the Beatles' Story or ride the Mersey ferry on a cold day.

Luckily, after that night's show I'd be going back on the helicopter with Felix. We would have two days off, and since I had no home to return to my plan was to learn more about the extraordinary home he had created for himself outside Stratford.

A first occurred in Liverpool. Those familiar with Felix's poetry might recall a little poem called

CLOCKWISE FROM TOP LEFT: Jack Hardy making another book sale · The audience at The Northumberland settle in · Toby Fisher on stage introducing Felix to yet another audience · Jerina Hardy, ready for work!

CLOCKWISE FROM TOP LEFT: Jack Hardy and Tom Rooke, the Merchandise Dream Team
· London guest poet, Pascale Petit meets Felix · Jamie Broome focuses for another show
· Nigel Ryan and Adrian Augier bringing Felix best wishes for the tour from world famous poet, Derek Walcott

CLOCKWISE FROM TOP LEFT: Benjamin Zephaniah, a surprise guest at the Milton Keynes event
· '3 down and 18 to go', Thom Stretton, Jamie Broome, Scott Watson and Mick Watson from Class Act · Busy book sales at The Northumberland

CLOCKWISE FROM TOP LEFT: Marie-France cross-stitching – her secret addiction
· Jonathan Noone, Wendy Kasabian and Caroline Rush become tourists for a couple of hours in Ludlow
· Felix signing, signing, signing · Whoops! – Another city, another parking ticket

CLOCKWISE FROM TOP LEFT: Jason Kersten and Jonathan Noone busy blogging · Sunset over Morecambe Bay as viewed from the helicopter · Bannams Wood, The Heart of England Forest

CLOCKWISE FROM TOP LEFT: Cardiff Guest Poet, Loveday Why gets a hug from Felix · Loveday Why with her husband, Chris
· The Class Act stage crew, Jamie Broome, Scott Watson, Mick Watson and Thom Stretton

CLOCKWISE FROM TOP LEFT: Felix and a fan: 'I must have signed a million books!' · Precision packing in the trailer
· Highfield, Felix's 'pleasure dome'

What else do rich tycoons do but build sculpture parks? To see it in person was a wondrous, fantastical experience. Again it came down to detail; the panes on the comic that R. Crumb was in the midst of drawing; the commands on Stephen Hawking's computer; the relaxed, conversational pose of Samuel Clemens, one of my three favourite authors, as he sat on a wooden bench. Strolling between the pieces of sculpture, I had that kid feeling again – a very well-read kid. Felix's worship of the classics, adventure and discovery was rampant. He also loved his country, which to me was supremely evident in the statue of three RAF pilots running towards their Spitfire planes. It belonged outside the Battle of Britain Museum, or in some square in London, which made it all the more extraordinary to see it sitting in the middle of the Warwickshire countryside.

'Children would love this place,' I told him. 'You could truck them in by the busload.'

'Already do. The local schoolkids come up here for field trips. Anyone who makes an appointment can visit.' That was always happening – me telling him things to do that he had seen to years earlier.

'What happens to Dorsington when you're gone?'

'Someone will buy it. It's a house.'

'And the garden? The statues should stay together.'

'They will. It will still be available to the public. Everything is being taken care of, Mr Kersten. I have a legion of people whose entire job is to see to it. What do you think I've spent the last ten years doing?'

Which brought us to the Heart of England Forest. Before I had finished my tea, he was making arrangements for Toby to meet me outside the Schoolhouse and take me to see one of his first plantings, Giddings Wood.

Constantly moving through towns and cities as we were, it was easy to forget one major purpose of the tour: raising money to plant trees. Sometimes when I watched Felix sign a book I imagined a sapling sprouting up from the earth, shaking the dirt off its little leaves, and squeaking, 'Thank you!' But unless you walk through the woods yourself the Heart of England Forest, or any forest for that matter, is all theoretical.

It was back in my Maxim days when I first heard that Felix was planting a 30,000-acre forest. In New York City, we had often wondered what he was doing with all that money we were making him. Our colleagues at other magazine empires such as Condé Nast and Hearst enjoyed gleaming new cafeterias and offices, lavish expense accounts and armies of assistants. Yet we were killing them in the marketplace with what Felix calls the labour force that matters: a skeleton staff of young, hungry and talented people who, when left alone in an environment with minimum supervision and maximum possibility, kick ass. But as profits rose, so did the speculation as to what the future held. I shall never forget a conversation I had with one naïve co-worker on the fourteenth floor of 1040 Avenue of the Americas.

'I think a big payoff could be headed our way,' he said. 'Think about it. He has no children, no wife. My theory is that he's planning on giving all of us a slice of the pie. Employee stock ownership.'

I held my laughter: it was nice seeing him dream. We all had little fantasies to help get us through the twenty-hour days. For my part, I was temporarily satisfied with a decent-paying job that allowed me the opportunity to do and learn all there was to know about magazines. I wrote and edited everything from crime features to gear reviews in which we tested products in highly unorthodox ways ('Your chainsaw may work great on wood. But how does it fare against a side of beef?'). Once I even hired a small, portable zoo of exotic animals, took them to Central Park and tested which species were best for picking up women. I was paid for this. (Bush babies, by the way, are pure chick magnets.)

I was in my third year at Maxim when the news spread that Felix had decided to leave his fortune to a forest. Some snickered that it was a predictable atonement for all the slaughtered trees. I actually thought it was brave: not only would he never get a single thank you from his sylvan beneficiaries, he wouldn't even be able to see its literal fruition. It was a leap of the imagination, a theoretical legacy that both assumed its value and reinforced it at the same time. It's a pretty safe bet that children will try to survive. He was betting that the world he left behind would take care of his voiceless children.

Toby dropped me off at the entrance to Giddings Wood with a backpack full of water, a couple of cans of beer and half a sandwich. The day was brilliant, clear and warm, and as I set off into fields of oak and elm and hazel and ash I felt the health that the bus had been sapping away return with the sunlight. This is how humans are supposed to live! I whipped off my shirt and trekked off madly into the trees. They were all about seven or eight feet high, saplings still, but tall enough to provide a positive feeling of isolation. Yet soon I became aware that I was not alone. Wrens and magpies called and there were a dozen rustlings in the knee-high grass. My mind wondered back to my childhood and to ancient, primeval ways of living. I wanted to explore, to have an adventure. 'I'm going to find a wooded stream and drink a beer next to it,' I decided.

The best hope for water was a line of tall trees on the far side of the wood. Felix creates footpaths in his woods so that people can stroll through, but to reach my chosen destination I would have to blaze my own trail between the saplings. Easy enough, I thought.

Five paces into the trees, I skidded to a halt in front of a web as big as a hockey goal. Inches from my face was a spider the size of a pocket watch. I backed up and detoured, only to immediately encounter another webby roadblock manned by yet another little nugget of menace. Screw Giddings Wood. He should have called it Spider Wood. At almost every turn was another web. It was a veritable arachnid jamboree ('Well, of course you saw spiders. It's spider season,' Felix later told me.) Determined not to let them stop me from reaching the stream, I picked up a stick and began carving my way through, making sure to disturb only webs that were unoccupied – and even those I snuck under when I could. Sixty-three days later, I reached the stream.

I enjoyed my beer thoroughly, then spent another hour exploring the woods, this time on the paths. What would this place look like in another ten years? Thirty? Barring biological or man-made disasters, it will remain for centuries. I imagined coming back a decade later with my daughter, explaining to her that the last time I'd strolled through was during a poetry tour featuring the same man who had planted these woods. I would tell her that, like one of those trees, I too had played a small part in creating Giddings Wood.

Giddings Wood in the Heart of England Forest

Felix Dennis 'The Bearded Dwarf' in the 90s

'The Mexicans will take it within your child's lifetime.'

'You sound like Nostradamus,' Kotok said.

'And within her child's lifetime, a state will once again secede from the Union,' he continued, unfazed. 'Do you know which one?'

'California.'

'That's right! Economically, they don't need the rest of the country, and they're far more progressive.'

I should have grilled him on how California could secede if it had already been reabsorbed into Mexico a generation earlier. Or, more currently, how our most debt-ridden state was going to get out of its present jam without some kind of federal aid or policy move. My native state had become America's Greece. Instead, I just asked him if he was willing to bet his entire fortune on this, with the cheque payable to my grandchildren.

'Of course,' he said. 'Unfortunately, I'll be dead before I can pay you. Ha ha ha ha ha!'

Dear Uncle Felix

Dear Uncle Felix,
I want to be rich like you,
A jet and yacht like the ones you've got.
What do I do?

Go and talk to your teacher.
Drown yourself in the moat.
The jet and the yacht I rent, you clot.
I enclose a five-pound note.

Dear Uncle Felix,
I want to be rich like you,
The fiver's spent but my bike is bent.
What do I do?

Sell yourself to a pervert.
Write to the police.
Do whatever you think is clever.
Here's twenty quid for some peace.

Dear Uncle Felix,
I want to be rich like you,
My girlfriend's preggers, we live like beggars,
What do I do?

Confess your sins to the vicar.
Subsist on bread and jam.
Batter the cat or eat your hat.
This fifty's for a pram.

Dear Uncle Felix,
I want to be rich like you,
For a thousand quid you'd be well rid
Of 'What do I do?'

Ah, blackmail is it, young 'un?
That's better— let me see.
I admire your cheek, next Monday week
Report to work for me!

With apologies and a respectful tip of a sheepish hat to Allan Ahlberg's
'Please Mrs. Butler' (Kestrel, 1983)

shouting, but also stamping the floor for more.

'You'll sell a lot of books tonight,' I told him during his pre-signing smoke break.

'No way – times are too rough,' he said. 'Plus, they were loud.' (An odd trend we'd noticed: the louder audiences usually bought fewer books.) But afterwards, Cork indeed set another record by purchasing more books per capita than any other city. These fine folks, among the hardest hit in Europe by the recession, gave more than anybody else. Gura míle maith agat indeed.

1960's counterculture, Sue had run Friends of Oz, the organisation that had supported the defendants during the obscenity trial. She was also a founder of Indica, the bookstore and art gallery where John Lennon met Yoko Ono. Later she went on to become an influential figure in London's restaurant scene.

I figured that the theme of the evening – hell, the tour – would end there, but out front during the book signing I met a young, recently unemployed actor who was reeling from a death too. Ed Mullane was a nice Irish kid, well spoken, a Felix fan. Since February he'd been touring Ireland in a play called God's Official, about two football players who kidnap an official over a bad call. The official was played by Mick Lally, a much-loved Irish actor best known for his role as a farmer in the soap opera Glenroe. For Mullane, working with Lally had been a breakout gig. Lally, like Felix, was sixty-three and a founder of one of the most respected theatre companies in Ireland, the Druid Theatre.

'This guy was so big,' Mullane told me. 'Every bar we'd go into people would buy him a drink. No one knew or gave a fuck who we were, but women were throwing their knickers at him. And he looked like a big farmer.'

Just a few weeks earlier, Mullane had gone out drinking with Lally after a show. Lally died later that night of a heart attack in his hotel room. Life over, tour over.

'I couldn't believe it,' Mullane said. 'You would have had no idea. It happened just like that.'

Definitely not the kind of story I'd share with Felix. When I popped back in to see how the signing was going, he was in a decent mood. A kid who can't have been older than fifteen was waiting in the queue with his father. In his hand were a couple of large glossy photos of a bearded Felix that were taken back in the Oz days.

'Good God, where did you get these?' he asked the boy when he approached to have Felix sign the photo.

'I printed them out from the Internet.'

'That's a first. Technically, I should get a piece of whatever you sell these for,' he said, his eyes narrowing as he signed them. 'But I admire your enterprise, lad! Just make sure you get a good price for them on eBay!'

The evening would have ended on an upbeat note if it weren't for a rambling drunk who'd been lingering outside the front doors. I'd exchanged a few words with him and he'd seemed harmless enough. He was a tall, dark-haired kid in his mid-twenties, a bit rangy. He wanted to know if Felix had any jobs available. I'd foolishly told him that if he bought a book and stood in line, he could ask Felix himself.

'I couldn't.'

'Sure you could. The man is very approachable,' I had said encouragingly.

Sure enough, he was the last guy in the queue. He must have swilled a few free glasses of liquid courage before buying a copy of Lone Wolf, because by the time he stood in front of Felix he was a blathering idiot.

'Mr. Dennis, can you please give me a job? Please, please! I'll do anything just to learn from you. I'll even work for free.'

'Sorry, mate. I'm employing too many people as it is. I'll sign this book for you, though. What would you like me to write?'

'Just your signature is fine,' he said, but then he made the mistake of returning to the line, which had grown by another two in the interim. 'I've changed my mind,' he told Felix, 'can you make it out to Mary?'

The spectacles began to steam. Felix bit his lip and was preparing to write 'Dear Mary' when the idiot pushed his luck. 'Actually, I don't even know anyone named Mary, I just think it would sound cool. What I really want is a job. C'mon, you must have something—'

'I am done with you. Leave me alone,' Felix said icily.

The fool just stood there in shock.

'I AM NOT YOUR PLAYTHING, SIR! GET OUT OF MY SIGHT!'

Adrian, who was standing to the side like a Praetorian guard, swooped in and gently escorted the guy away from the table, sternly suggesting that it was time for him to go. He left ashen and confused.

'One thing I will not do is suffer fools,' Felix explained when I looked at him with wide eyes. 'They are thieves who steal time.'

They steal more than that. The guy walked off with Felix's Yoropen, worth a good £30.

The lights of Dublin whizzed past the tour bus's window. All too soon we were back in the port, stacked up with the horde of trucks waiting to cross that little sea that feels like an ocean. We left Ireland as we had come, dog tired, in the dead of night, with a French stowaway.

It was hard to believe that the tour was now more than half over. Before us was a two-day break (count them!) in London. It would be followed by the final and most gruelling leg: six days of performances in a row. But before returning to London we needed to drop the Class Act boys back at their headquarters, and this was something I had been keen on seeing. They spent so much time on the road that wherever they called home had to be special. And when Mick slid open the doors to his warehouse in a village near Aylesbury, I wasn't disappointed.

Inside was a wonderland: a company of life-sized and larger-than-life-sized figures that Mick had accumulated over the years for themed events. Strolling through, I saw James Dean, a spacesuit-clad astronaut planting an American flag, a Dalek, various dinosaurs, Elvis Presley, a pair of jousting knights on horseback, Abbott and Costello, an alien smoking a cigar, a set of life-size Oscar statues, a 'Welcome to Fabulous Las Vegas' sign, the Blues Brothers, the Rat Pack singing, a dozen cowboys and Indians and at least a dozen pirates all with the appropriate paraphernalia like tepees and treasure chests, Ronald McDonald, a private detective, Frankenstein's monster, a gorilla, polar bears, Michael Jordan, a conquistador, Zorro, Al Capone, American GIs, and a Japanese garden pagoda with a bridge. These were just the most visible; on ramparts above and stuffed into inaccessible corners were countless other figures large and small.

'Started out in screen printing,' Mick later explained as he sat behind his desk in an office filled with old movie posters. 'I'd been asked by a production company to do some labels and badges. Went in there to deliver them, noticed what they did, and offered my services as a rigger. I ended up being his manager for a year. And then I thought I could do the job better, so I started this company. Started off with fifty quid – I borrowed that. I'm still skint, but I've got a lot of equipment.'

He had accumulated his army of props over the years, as clients – corporate ones mainly – hired him for themed events: Oscar parties, Vegas nights, Halloween bashes… You name it, he could not only prop it but light it, stage it, sound it. Opposite the props was a stack of speakers and audio-visual equipment ten feet high. Sadly, interest in props was slacking off, thanks to the rise of digital display. He had just bought a massive LED screen, and more was coming.

'It's just costing thousands a year to store it, and it's not selling,' he said of the mannequin crowd. 'Probably gonna sell off an awful lot of it and invest that into more sound and lighting. It's a shame, because theming is fun. Hard work, but imaginary land is good.'

I imagined the sad goodbyes as Godzilla bade farewell to Roy Rogers and the Blues Brothers fought back tears as the Rat Pack were loaded into crates and trundled off towards whoever bought them on eBay. I hoped all would find appreciative homes. Felix's tree trunk podium, which Mick had lovingly created out of resin and paint, would no doubt join the throng, perhaps to be picked up for a gatekeeper at a national park or a group of garden party lovers.

though in those days there wasn't much choice. The Great War had decimated the male population of the working-class neighbourhood they lived in, Gorgie, and many of those who came back alive had to look after the children of their dead brothers and friends. My grandmother lived in a two-bedroom flat without hot water and with seven other people, most of them kids. Raymond's mum, her cousin, was one of those kids. Like Felix, my grandmother was a devotee of classical and popular poetry, and years later she wrote a poem about her childhood called 'Tea Time'.

> The children are jumping rope, singing skip and go songs
> Dresses flapping like washing on the line.
> Shrill, young voices chanting the old, old rhymes.
>
> The evening is upon us now as doors and windows slam.
> It's time to drop the rope; it's time for tea and jam.
>
> The working dads are coming home from a day of heavy toil.
> The fires burn bright, the tables set, the kettles puff and boil.
>
> Footsteps on the stairway, a scrape upon the mat –
> The children jump for joy, and fight for Daddy's lap.
>
> In another house along the way, the children wait for tea,
> A mother beside the hearth, an infant on her knee.
>
> The mantelpiece is shining with candlesticks of brass,
> A little box of medals enshrined within a glass;
>
> A picture of a soldier, handsome and carefree.
> And a parchment from the Monarch – 'He died for Liberty.'

It couldn't have been easy growing up in that other 'house along the way', but I never once heard her complain. 'I had a wonderful time growing up with my cousins,' she once told me. 'For entertainment, we read to each other every night and sang songs. If you are bored in this world, it is nobody's fault but your own.'

Home life got even more difficult when her mother died of an unknown illness when she was just fifteen, but my grandmother kept up her schooling. Inspired by Elsie Inglis, the 'Florence Nightingale' of Scotland, she trained as a nurse. When war broke out again in 1939 she enlisted in the Royal Air Force, where she met my Yank grandfather, Marion Johnston. Their romance is another story, but suffice it to say that once he took her back to America the lines of relationship back to Edinburgh blurred with time and distance. By the time I was born my grandmother had been away from Scotland for almost thirty years, but it never left her. She sang me and my cousins Scottish lullabies, joined the local clan club and always spoke warmly of her home country. She was Scottish and damn proud of it. When my mother handed me her ashes in 2004, there was no question as to what I would do with them. The only uncertainties were how and when.

I quickly emailed Raymond back, letting him know that I was eager to meet him and all my relations in Edinburgh. Provided, of course, that I survived the rest of the tour.

I mentioned earlier that on any given day Felix's mood is public knowledge among all his employees. On the day of our second show in London, the forecast was grim. He wasn't feeling well and, to Jerina's horror, had cancelled an interview with BBC One at the last minute. Rumour had it that, instead of resting, he had stayed up all night writing poetry. Worst of all, the storm was headed my way. He was angry at me for not updating his Facebook page, a task he had handed to me for the duration of the tour.

'I had two days off,' I explained to Caroline. She just shrugged. My days off were irrelevant. I would still have to bear the wrath.

For those curious about what Felix can be like when he's angry, the faint of heart need not apply. Profanities, base insults centred on your stupidity, frightening volume levels – a tsunami with an English accent. Don't bother looking for allies – they've gone for high ground. The upside is that passive aggression isn't part of his emotional arsenal. You know where you stand the second you are in his presence. So as I watched him get out of the Maybach behind London's Shaw Theatre, I was braced and ready. He took one look at me standing at the back door, opened his mouth, and started…singing.

'I'm a yankee doodle dan-dee, I'm a yankee doodle boy….'

So much for the Felix forecast.

'Is it true you stayed up all night writing?' I asked him.

'That is absolutely right,' he said. 'I have a new poem, and you're going to hear it tonight.'

He was positively ebullient. We had a full house of almost 450, which included a group of some of his oldest and dearest friends. Backstage that night were two legends: Don Atyeo and Boss Goodman. Don was the former Oz editor who had co-written Bruce Lee: King of Kung-Fu, the book that had launched Dennis Publishing. He'd gone on to a stellar career. Boss Goodman was a famous club manager and former roadie. As Felix put it, 'There isn't a single great band in England who doesn't know him.'

You can always tell good friends by how badly they behave together. When Don and Boss enquired about the tour, Felix made sure he let them know what they were missing.

'A woman in Leeds tried to sneak under the table and suck my dick.'

'I bet she tripped and fell on her head,' said Don.

'Ask Jerina Hardy. There were young girl admirers too.'

'Define young at our age.'

'Under twenty-five.'

'Ooooh,' both Don and Boss jeered.

'Don, you think I am joking. I am not joking.'

'Okay, I'll come backstage later.'

'Yeah. You can have the leftovers. Ha ha ha ha ha!'

Talk soon turned to the missing musketeer, Mick Farren. The frontman for the Deviants and Pink Fairies, sci-fi author and grandfather of punk rock, he was the most famous of them all from the Oz days. In Japan, he is still worshipped by young girls for hits such as 'Vampires Stole My Lunch Money' and 'Lex Luthor Supermarket'.

'Micky can't sing,' Felix explained, 'and his whole idea was, I'm the lead singer of the Fairies and I can't fucking sing. And, he'd just shout into the microphone. And of course, he was the grandfather of punk because he was doing it long before anyone else. He understood how unnecessary it was to be able to play a musical instrument, including singing.'

Felix recalled paying for Mick's wedding back in the 1980s, a grand and decadent affair next to the Russian consulate in the smart London district of Kensington. 'Everyone had to wear white. All the Fairies were coming and they had to match the cocaine. No one would touch the cake because it was full of acid. It was shaped like a girl with big knockers, and the knockers were full of acid.'

After spending decades in California, in two weeks Mick was due to return and settle in Brighton.

'He'll be able to moan and whine about England's weather constantly on his blog,' Felix said. 'It'll be great for him.' The one hold up was his cat. To sidestep British customs, he'd been talking about giving the feline some Demerol and sneaking it through in a bag. Though no one was certain if that would even be possible, the real concern was the Demerol. 'We're afraid Mick will take it all and be the one passed out when the plane lands,' Felix said to the great laughter of the others.

'Ah, Mick,' Felix wound up. 'You know you're a legend when you've got appreciation websites when you're alive. Know what I mean? You and me, Boss, we've got no appreciation'. There are, in fact, several appreciation websites devoted to Boss Goodman.

After his two friends returned to the auditorium, Felix showered them with praise. He told a story of how Boss Goodman had called him up and urged him to sign a particular band for the Dennis Publishing Christmas party. They were charging only £25, so Felix signed them. In between the signing and the party, they became the number one band in Britain. On the night of the party, all the streets had to be blocked off around Kingly Street. The band was Dire Straits.

'There wasn't a single member of Dennis Publishing down there,' he lamented. 'They'd all scalped the tickets!'

'How come we never got a party like that?' I asked.

'You didn't have Boss Goodman, that's why. The answer was standing in front of you – a legend in his own lunchtime.'

Don, who could take the piss out of a four thousand-year-old Egyptian mummy, had a meteoric career after being Felix's partner. He had gone on to become the most successful editor of Time Out, where he was equally famous for splitting the coffee cup of one of his columnists with a samurai sword during a meeting. He wound up heading back to Hong Kong to run two highly successful TV stations, while his wife, Susan, ran Ted Turner's Cartoon Network. Don had been offered piles of money to stay in television, but, unlike Felix, he had retired early, at fifty-one.

'He left the game with a few million and never looked back,' Felix said appreciatively. 'He thinks I'm mad. He's the only guy I know who thoroughly enjoys retirement. Not remotely interested in working – couldn't give a shit.' Don now spent half his time as the executor of Felix's literary estate; the other half he spent in Mustique, where he watched over Shogun, the exquisite house next door to Mandalay that Felix rented out for up to $50,000 a week.

I couldn't help marvelling at these two kids who had co-written those biographies all those years ago, then ridden the waves of success to very different places. It was the partnership of a lifetime. Could there have been one without the other?

Felix's second show in London was Big – there was no other word for it. With a sellout crowd in the Shaw Theatre and many of his closest friends in the audience, he decided to go for broke. 'I have a special feeling about tonight,' he told the audience at the outset. Then he proceeded to do something I'd never seen him do before: he had fun.

It wasn't so much that the recitals were different (although he did the best rendition of 'The Bearded Dwarf' I've seen yet); it was that in between poems he smiled, and talked to the audience in an unrehearsed way. By the end of the first set they were having the time of their lives and hitting the wine, hard. When it was time for the second set, Jonathan Noone noticed a man sitting by himself surrounded by empty glasses. He ordered the wine to be taken away from all the tables to encourage him to return to his seat.

'Why did you have the wine cleared?' the man asked.

'The second half is about to commence,' he replied.

The man stared at him in a haze, then said, 'You fucking asshole.' Jonathan was going to have none of this. 'Well, fuck you too,' he said. 'Would you like to leave?' It was the one threat that always worked. The drunkard finally sulked away.

A few poems into the second set, Felix abandoned his usual script entirely, and between recitals ruminated on the tour's enduring theme: aging and mortality. He directed his message to the younger members of the audience.

'I hate it. I loathe it and I detest it. I make accommodation. We all do. But my God! If they handed me a babe I'd never met and told me I could suck its brains out and live for another fifty years... And would you say no? And within thirty years or forty years, that's what they will be telling you. So people of my generation might not be tempted, but you will. You will. That's what will happen with science. And good luck to you. And I'm glad I won't be here.'

The crowd was electrified. 'Did he just say that?' a woman whispered when the baby brains line came up. But she and everyone else was riveted. Near the end of the second set, Felix seemed almost to fall into a trance. It was time to read his new poem.

'And now I'd like to try something dangerous, something I think performers ought not to do,' he said. 'I wish to read you a poem I have never read in public. I've never read it for a very simple reason: I wrote it last night. It was a cold, damp night in Warwickshire last night, the first taste of winter in the south Midlands. I was feeling unwell, a little tired. I was exhausted from this tour. With a sharp pain in my left side – kidneys or knotted back, I don't know which – congested bronchial system and other ailments. And I was alone. I was in no mood to write or do anything but pile logs on the fire and feel sorry for myself. Hours passed. I couldn't even be bothered to go to bed. I sat in my great red velvet chair. So many friends have died recently, one just this week. And my thoughts were with them. And then I realised that my melancholy was getting out of hand – not to mention that the reflection of self-pity in a mirror is not exactly an edifying sight. So I deliberately altered the course of my thoughts. I remembered how lucky I had been. How lucky I am. How the love of another, and my discovery of poetry, has steered me from a propensity to play handstands on the roof of hell, not much caring whether I slipped or not. I fell asleep at three o'clock, then woke. And though I did not wish to, I climbed up the stairs to my chilly study, my mind warm with almost perfect lines with what I knew would make a sonnet. Within the hour it was done. I toyed with it and reversed a word here or there until long after the grey dawn. And in essence, it wrote itself. And now I will do a dangerous thing and share it with you.'

The World Is As It Is

The world is as it is, not as it seems –
While troubadours of blood profess their tale
Our senses breed conspiracies of dreams
To weave a very necessary veil.
So Nature in her wisdom shields our sight,
The scale of what is Other screened from view,
'Til, by degrees, we cast a faltering light
On mysteries whose face we never knew.
Thus love itself exposes what was hid:
We met – the earth was flat – love made it round;
Love grew – we lost our feet – and as we slid
Each mountain we had climbed shrunk to a mound.
    Who claims that love is blind plays blind man's buff:
    While those who claim to see, love not enough.

To A Beautiful Lady Of A Certain Age

Lady, lady do not weep —
What is gone is gone. Now sleep.
Turn your pillow, dry your tears,
Count thy sheep and not thy years.

Nothing good can come of this.
Time rules all, my dearest,'tis
But folly to be waging war
On one who never lost before.

Lady, this is all in vain,
Youth can never come again;
We have drunk the summer wine,
None can make a stitch in time.

Nip and tuck 'til crack of doom,
What is foretold in the womb
May not be forsworn with gold —
Nor may time be bought or sold.

Dearest, do I love thee less,
Do I shrink from thy caress?
Think you I could cease to care?
Never was there one so fair!

Lady, lady do not weep —
What is gone is gone. Now sleep.
Lean against me, calm your fears,
Count thy blessings, not thy years.

Addiction

I can't.
You can't? We both know what we need.
I CAN'T!
You see? The tiger needs to feed.

I won't.
You will... we both know how it stands.
I WON'T!
Why not? There's no one understands.

Get out.
To where? I live inside your head.
Get OUT!
No dice. I'll sleep when I've been fed.

Shut up.
I have. That's you you're listening to.
Shut UP!
Oh boy. Just wake me when you're through.

Not now.
Uh huh. We've been through this before.
NOT NOW!
Uh huh. The stuff is in the drawer.

It hurts.
Of course. The biter's being bit.
It HURTS!
Me too. Now get us both a hit.

Just one.
Yeah, sure— one goddam motherlode.
Just ONE!
Just one. And one more for the road.

True Love

True love shoulders any weight,
  Soldiering in secret mazes,
Shreds the wire and scales the gate,
  Blind to disapproving gazes.
Shut out— true love battles through.
(And if it fail, it was not true.)

True love's warrant knows no border,
  Forging visas, bribing guards,
Feral, like some crazed marauder
  Practising absurd charades.
Thwarted— true love turns the screw.
(And if it fail, it was not true.)

True love shames the rising sun
  Laughing at its feeble heat;
In that glare, strange deeds are done,
  Love knows nothing of defeat.
Banished— true love plots anew.
(And if it fail, it was not true.)

CHAPTER EIGHTEEN
WARWICK

The Bridgehouse
Theatre

280

152

Michael Hulse

from To My Father

(VIII)

Blown off the Wall by Easter wind and rain,
we're sheltering in the lee of a lonely farm,
no other sign of comfort or of warmth
in all Northumberland, for all I know,

and you, with your nose in your precious book,
ferreting out a passage again
in your tattered vade mecum,
the indispensable Collingwood Bruce,

you tell me that a hundred years ago
the chives once planted by the legion
stationed here at Walltown
were growing in the grasses still, sixteen centuries on.

God knows I'm used to hearing things like this.
My childhood has been spent in other ages,
a game of hide-and-seek in ancient ruins.
My family includes the Roman Empire.

And so I'm unsurprised by what comes next.
Chives, you announce, are indestructible.
If they were here a century ago,
they'll be here still. We only have to look.

Of course I look at the field and think you're mad.
I'm soaked and cold and all I see is grass.
But no — you're a boy. A husband, father, man — but still a boy.
Like me, your son. We are two boys together.

And when at last, exulting, and unchastened by the weather,
we find the chives in the wild wet grass, and in my quickened mind
I see the Iberian legionnaire
who planted herbs of home away from home,

the world has undergone a change —
to live in time is to grasp the hand
of a man at his work in a kitchen garden,
a man long dead but no more dead than you are, Dad, today.

Michael Hulse
From *The Secret History* (Arc, 2009)

18 Warwick

The Bridgehouse Theatre · 280 in attendance · 152 bottles consumed · guest poet Michael Hulse

Regardless of clichés, there are certain tasks every American is required to perform in England. One of them is to stand in front of Buckingham Palace and try to make the Queen's Guard crack a smile. (My brother and I had attempted this years earlier and, after hammering them with every obscenity and dirty joke we could muster, walked away feeling ashamed.) Another is to walk across Abbey Road like the Beatles. Despite numerous visits to England, I had never completed one of the most important requirements: visiting a proper English castle.

'There aren't that many proper castles left, but you're in luck,' Caroline informed me early in the tour. 'Warwick Castle is one of the best preserved.' As a local girl, she knew, so after lunch that day I tramped off towards the ramparts to fulfil my touristic destiny. From the surrounding streets, the castle indeed looked like everything you'd expect: high turrets, imposing walls, a moat. Then I reached the entrance.

Twenty-five quid!

I didn't care if King Arthur himself was waiting on the other side to knight me, it was an outrageous amount to charge a guest. The closest comparison we have in America – and I cringe to say it – is probably Graceland. Elvis's home, which is much better preserved and heated, costs $31 to visit, which at that time was equivalent to about £17 or £18. I stood in indignant disbelief near the turnstile, which was conspicuously located in the gift shop, waiting for someone to offer me a Yank discount or direct me to a cheaper Yank entrance. Oddly, I couldn't see anyone, which made me wonder if today was maybe a free day. No one was manning the ticket booth. The first and only person I saw was a young mother with a crying baby who passed me as she left the castle through a flimsy gate. It swung open and hung there provocatively. Without hesitation, I stepped in.

I half expected someone to shackle me and haul me off to a dungeon, but all was quiet. As I stepped out on to the grounds, I saw why: the ticket taker was having a smoke just past the entrance. If he did think about confronting me, he must have decided it was too late in the day to bother. That is how this lone Yank successfully conquered one of England's most famous castles, for free.

Conquered is too strong a word. Warwick Castle, I learned as soon as I entered the interior, had clearly already been taken by Madame Tussaud's, who bought it in 1978. Animatronic horses, campy soundtracks of howls and screams, wax figures of goitred peasants and well-dressed princes going about their medieval business – Tussaud's has done a marvellous job of annihilating any imagery that might spring from the human imagination in such a magnificent place. The most interesting object I saw there was an old stone toilet; it was the only feature not marred by some garish doll, allowing me to wonder how many towering historical figures had planted their royal behinds upon that very spot and dropped cannonballs – everyone from William the Conqueror to Edward IV to Queen Elizabeth had probably shat there. In fact, a few minutes later I would learn just how important that little commode was.

Touristic duties required me to climb to the castle's highest point – Caesar's Tower. I was recovering my breath up there, admiring the ramparts and countryside by myself, when I felt a tectonic shift in my intestines. The road diet had caught up with me. My last four meals had been a Big Mac, some bad pizza, a doughnut and finally some French onion soup, the last of which I had deluded myself into thinking would help combat The Cough. This witches' brew had hit critical mass. I knew that my visit was over; I needed to find a peasant toilet, pronto.

The dilemma, which I could clearly survey from the tower, was that the nearest facilities were a good two hundred yards away. At the same time, there was a closer exit that offered a much faster return to the venue. If I could hold things together just a little longer, I reasoned, I'd be able to do my business in privacy and save a little time.

Halfway back to the venue, the pressure in my nether regions was literally causing me to sweat. It was unlike any sphincteric reflex I had ever experienced. I fought it off with stomach-clenching, jaw-grinding, and puckering action, but it was as persistent as a baby, with contractions increasing in force and frequency. Just past an old bridge, I spotted some woods with a 'No Trespassing' sign. My panick-stricken mind calculated: if I ran into those woods and crouched, would anyone see me? What would happen if I got caught in the act? An arrest? No, I'd make it unseen – but the real problem was no toilet paper. I studied the foliage, wishing I had Felix's knowledge of trees. For all I knew, half that greenery was some strange English version of poison oak. No, best hold it together. You're in England, be stoic and endure.

Running was not an option. I knew that the moment I shook the brew, it would become as volatile as nitroglycerine. Returning to my colleagues having shit my pants was unthinkable. I could breathe a thousand years and never live it down. It would be the only thing any of these wonderful people would remember of me, especially the publisher of the Viz magazine's swearing dictionary Magna Farta.

Lack of facilities wasn't the worst problem. Just past the wood was a fork in the road. I had forgotten which way I'd come. Truly the forces of my own body were lined up against me. Wasting no time, I called Caroline and begged hastily for directions.

'Hi Caroline it's Jason don't mean to bother you just a little lost I just passed the bridge can you tell me which way to go?'

'Do you see a football field?'

'Uh no.'

'Oh, I'm sorry, I meant tennis courts.'

Football field? Tennis courts? No, I didn't see any of that. It was all fading into a confusing green and grey haze of trees and streets – the dizziness that no doubt accompanies the manic breakdown that precedes the moment right before you poop your pants for the first time since you were three. This was it. I wasn't going to make it.

Just then I heard two horn beeps behind me. It was Lloyd! Save the birth of my daughter, I have never been so glad to see another human being. He was doing his recce in one of Felix's Rolls Royces. I hung up on Caroline, jumped into the front seat and told him to step on it and why. He rocketed me back to the venue within forty seconds. The hardest part was not running the last twenty yards to the toilet. It's a wonder the walls of Warwick Castle still stand after the ensuing blast.

Such was my relief at surviving this ordeal that I had to tell someone, so a few minutes later I mentioned it to Mick. His eyes went wide in disbelief.

'You won't believe this, Jason, but I swear to God the same thing happened to me coming back from that fucking town,' he said. 'You say you thought about using the wood?'

'Yes.

'The one just past the bridge?'

'That was it.'

'There was a little fence.'

'I thought about jumping it.'

'By the golf course.'

'So that's what it was.'

'My God, Mick! When I finally reached the loo here—'

'It came out of there like a Japanese gunboat!' he laughed. 'We must be getting old.'

The tour was breaking all of us by then. Even the unflappable Marie-France, who could keep her cool on the surface of the sun, was getting fatigued.

'I'm tired of this thing,' she said around that time. 'I want to go home.'

'Why don't you?' I asked her. 'All you have to do is ride back on the helicopter with Felix.' A jacuzzi and a sauna every night. A swim in Highfield's mermaid pool, a nice home-cooked meal, a warm fire. My God, a good sleep! All she had to do was ask.

'No way. He told me that I wouldn't last a week on the bus. I won't give him the satisfaction.' I was relieved to hear this, because the bus wouldn't have been the same without her. The few occasions on which somebody had managed to sneak home for a night, they were missed. We had become, to my surprise, a unit. Continuing the tour without everybody on board was unimaginable.

Even though Felix returned home every night, he faced his own deprivations. Most of us were done working by the time he got home, but there were no tour-brothers-in-arms or after-show party waiting for him back at the Old Manor – just isolation and the proverbial golden bars. Backstage visitors would take one look at his schedule and start using words like 'brutal' and 'gruelling'.

Sooner or later, the man has to crash, I thought to myself as I waited for Felix at the theatre door in Warwick. Following the previous night's marathon performance in London, he'd had a late Chinese dinner with friends and no one had heard anything from him all day.

Sure enough, he arrived later than normal, looking haggard and tired. His back, which had been bothering him for a week, was still hurting him. Despite negative test results, he was certain it was some sort of fatal kidney ailment. 'It ain't my muscles,' he said grimly as he shuffled up the backstage ramp. 'I haven't pulled any muscles. So that's what it will be, then. No use rationalising that, when you're sixty-three, muscles do weird things for no apparent reason. '

For the first time on the tour, he forewent his pre-show wine in favour of coffee, which he used to knock back a couple of Ibuprofen. Facing six nights in a row, he began brooding on a way to make it easier. The problem was that his helicopter would not save him from the impending inconveniences of Scotland: Glasgow's helipad was over an hour outside the city, and there wouldn't even be a chopper available to take him from Dorsington to Edinburgh. Somebody else had reserved it.

'I'm still looking at fucking Scotland,' he groaned. 'Toby, can you call the helicopter people and check flight times from Glasgow and Edinburgh? Their suggestion was that they fly me in to Birmingham airport, get a tiny little private jet – doesn't even have to be a jet, it could be a propeller – that's his argument, it would be much quicker.'

All this sounded confusing. A plane as opposed to the chopper? To me, that meant only one thing: no helo for grandma's ashes.

'Does this mean that the helicopter won't be available in Edinburgh?' I asked him.

'No no, don't worry about it,' he snapped, immediately smelling my worry. 'It will all get done. And we're just talking about me, so I don't give a fuck about you.' It was the closest thing to a harsh tone he'd taken with me the entire trip. But he immediately calmed down and reassured me that my grandmother's ashes would be delivered as planned.

Deciding to make myself scarce, I wandered out front to see how the crowd was shaping up. One of the first people I saw was Steve Rosenfield, who was talking to a man who was a dead ringer for Mick Jagger. His name was Mark Bosch, and he was a professional guitar player of note. He'd recently been touring with Ian Hunter, and he'd spent most of his adult life touring with rock and roll bands all over the world – and he looked it. In addition to being a Jagger doppelganger he had the skinny, angular appendages of a guitar man, and he wore a black fedora with a feather in it.

'I brought Mark in case you need to learn some additional bus – what's the right word? – etiquette?' Rosenfeld said. 'This is a guy who knows how to be on the bus.'

'Any tips on how to survive?' I asked Bosch.

'Do you get enough wine on the bus?'

'Tons. It's everywhere. We're brushing our teeth with it.'

'Good. A couple of bottles, and everyone hits the bunk.'

'I think we need more pills.'

'I've got Tylenol PMs if you need them.'

'Thanks. Wouldn't hurt.'

He reached into his shirt pocket and handed me four blue pills.

'Don't ask what's in his other pocket!' Rosenfeld snickered.

In his other pocket were in fact a mild variety of magic mushrooms. He had picked them himself some days earlier, behind a hotel in a large English city. Mushrooms always grow in the same place, and for years travelling musicians from all over the world had harvested them, not unlike migrating birds returning to the same berry bush. Life on tour was enhanced by just such secrets, and every town had them.

'Want to see the bus?' I asked him, though in retrospect it seemed a silly question. He had seen more buses than a Greyhound station. I wanted to see how Das Boot stood up, and he was happy to humour me. We trooped out back behind the stage and into the rear parking area. Once inside, he inspected the kitchen, lounge and sleeping compartments with a discerning eye.

'I've been on a bus exactly like this,' he finally declared. 'This is a good bus. With this many people travelling on it, you won't find better.'

We went back outside and had a smoke. It was a relief to be hanging out with a stranger who knew exactly what I was going through. He took one look at the tour schedule printed on the trailer and whistled.

'You must be dazed at this point,' he said. 'I bet you can't wait to get back to Smith Street.'

'How did you know I was from Brooklyn?'

'I took a guess.' It was a damn good one, considering that I live less than half a mile from Smith Street.

Musicians, poets, stage actors – travelling performers of any kind – were all one clan, I realised, the Brotherhood of the Show. It didn't matter what you did. You lived in buses and hotel rooms and you moved on. Yesterday was always a thousand years and miles ago. Touring for six months straight, as Mark Bosch had done, seemed incomprehensible to me, but at the same time I already knew how it was done; you surrendered, and the fewer ties you had the better.

'You know, I thought I'd lose weight on this tour,' I told him, 'what with all the irregular meals and movement. But I've gained at least five pounds.'

'Nah, you never lose weight on tour,' he laughed. 'Too much shitty road food and too much alcohol. Don't even worry about it, bro.'

For all his aches and tiredness, Felix's first set was surprisingly good that night in Warwick. Not the best I'd seen – though Mick actually thought it was his best first set so far – but still damn entertaining. During the interval, a couple of school friends of Felix's, Peter and Jennie Quesnel, joined us backstage. They were beaming, impressed and clearly proud of their old friend.

'And you saw no sign of this when you were kids?' I asked them when Felix was distracted by another guest.

'Oh, God, yes,' Quesnel answered emphatically.

'What did you see?'

'He just had this miraculous gift of being able to recite poetry and pieces of literature,' said Jennie.

Felix's story about discovering his gift while in hospital had never rung quite true to me. Although he swore by the story, which had been printed in almost every profile of him over the last decade, he was too passionate and clever at his craft for it to have simply sprung from nowhere. I had long suspected that he had been a closet poet his whole life. It made perfect sense, especially when you factored in his early days as an R&B singer, a young romantic looking for avenues of expression. The world saw him as a business tycoon dabbling in high art, but from the perspective of his youth he was simply picking up where he'd left off when he threw himself into commerce. Spiritually, Felix was a poet who had spent forty years dabbling in business and was now making up for lost time.

'So did he actually write poetry back in high school?' I asked Quesnel, hoping for some physical evidence.

'He just sent me a photocopy of our school magazine from 1964,' he said, 'And he's got two poems in it.'

Jackpot. I made plans for Quesnel to try to get me copies of the poems later. (Despite several attempts to relocate this issue, from the St Nicholas Grammar School for Boys, at present it is still 'missing in action'. No doubt somebody out there has a copy, though it is uncertain whether or not Felix wants the world to see it!)

'So you're seeing something you've seen your whole life?'

'Well, he used to do it,' Quesnel said thoughtfully, 'but now he is it.'

I figured that Felix would either cruise along through the second set, or lose steam and fall back on workmanlike deliveries. Given the consistently high level of performances he'd been firing off since the tour began, who could fault him? Since Warwick was only twenty minutes from his home in Dorsington, a home town crowd full of well-wishers was exactly the sort of audience that would accept good over great. No one informed him of that, however, because his second set was easily the best I'd seen. Poems that normally don't do much for me, like 'True Love', caught my ear as if I'd been hearing them for the first time. He wasn't merely reciting them, but feeling them, on a night when he should have been in bed. Mick Watson saw this too, and after the performance we met Felix in the dressing room to give him the good news.

'Where did that come from?' I asked Felix.

'It didn't come from me,' he said. 'It came from the audience. I had nothing to do with it.'

Love Came to Visit Me

Love came to visit me,
   Shy as a fawn,
But finding me busy, she
   Fled with the dawn.

At twenty, the torch of
Resentment was lit,
My rage at injustice
Waxed hot as the pit,
The flux of its lava
Cleared all in its path,
Comrades and enemies
Fled from its wrath.
Yet lovers grew wary
Once novelty waned —
To lie with a panther
Is terror unfeigned.

At thirty, my powers
Seemed mighty to me,
The fruits of my rivals
I shook from the tree,
By guile and by bluster,
By night and by day,
I battered and scattered
The fools from my way;
And women grew willing
To sham and to bluff —
Their trinkets and baubles
Cost little enough.

From forty to fifty,
I sought the abyss,
Each concubines' laughter
As false as her kiss.
We feasted and revelled
And rutted in muck,
Forgetting our peril,
Forgetting to duck,
Forgetting time's arrows
Are sharper than knives,
Grown sick of our swagger —
And sick of our lives.

Then came a miracle.
Loving but stern,
A Muse I knew naught of
Chided me: 'Turn!
Thy towers are faithless
And built upon sand,'
Then haltered and helpless
And led by the hand
I wandered in byways
Of shadow and light,
And seeing no help for it,
Sat down to write.

Love came to visit me,
    Shy as a fawn,
But finding me busy, she
    Fled with the dawn.

'I am listening, now...'

I am listening, now. The past is past,
I'm here. I'm sitting beside your bed.
Speak to me now. It's time at last
To make amends. The past is dead.

I am listening, now. I'm here, my dear.
Your spotted hands are soft as fur.
Speak to me, now. I've ears to hear,
They are not so deaf as once they were.

I am listening, now. I'm done with fuss;
Babble of treachery, love or pain,
Speak of yourself, of them, of us—
Speak of the ghosts that fill the rain.

I am listening, now. I left it late,
Later than ever we thought or knew.
Speak to me. Please. Unbar the gate.
Turn back, my dear. I'm here for you.

Perfect Day

Today was one of the best days of my life.
Nothing of any importance occurred—
I cut my finger on a paperknife
And marvelled at a busy hummingbird
Plucking out wet moss by a waterfall;
Broke bread with friends and shared a glass of wine;
Wrote this poem; swam; made love. That's all.
Why should it be some days erect a shrine,
A cairn, a white stone day, in memory?
Is it, as Buddhists claim, a lack of need,
Or want— or simple serendipity —
The perfect flowering of one small seed?
   The wise will say our frames are none too pure:
   How many perfect days could we endure?

CHAPTER TWENTY ONE
WINDERMERE

The Low Wood Hotel

179

153

Helen Mort

How To Leave The Stage

'There are more ways to leave the room
than the door and the window' – Don Paterson

Dive through a letterbox. Burn your farewell note.
Ascend the hero's leg, jump down the villain's throat.
Slip underneath a doormat with the long-discarded post
or hitch your way out to the lonely coast.
Set down your wine bottle, then vanish down its neck
or shimmy through the floorboards of an old shipwreck.
Wear only black. Adopt a different name.
Travel in the pocket of your oldest flame.
Disguise yourself as someone who you haven't met.
Retrace old routes you swore that you'd forget.
Taper through the holes in a white string vest
or ride the sun as it slinks down into the west.
And should you ever feel the urge to stay, be quick and deft -
discard your promises stage right, your heart stage left.

Helen Mort

Glasgow
The Òran Mór · 250 in attendance · 192 bottles consumed · guest poet Ailie MacDonald

As Thom Stretton illustrated, there is a natural tendency to let oneself go after living three weeks on a tour bus. Following the show in Windermere, Mick refused to allow him back on the bus unless he showered. Thom returned to us shiny-headed and glum, having lost his battle with entropy. Unknowingly, he had also provided me with my retort pastiche, based on Felix's poem 'I Am Listening Now'. Here's an extract from it.

I Am Smelling You Now

I am smelling you now. That scent is your scent,
I'm sure. I'm choking by your bunk.
Wash for me now. It's time you rent
Three days' sweat. That awful funk.

I am smelling you, now. You bathed too late
Later than we ever thought or knew.
Bathe for me. Please. Be a good mate.
Scrub your back, my dear. God, am I smelling you.

Stret's lapse in personal hygiene had made choosing the theme all too easy. But he would not be the only one on the tour who surrendered civilised norms in favour of convenience.

At some point, Marie-France decided that the immediate world outside the bus was really just a giant extension of our living quarters. She would step out of the bus in slippers or pyjamas, her hair witching out, and walk into a coffee shop or a restaurant, then brush her teeth in the loo, ignoring everyone, and return to the bus. When you know you're leaving a place within twenty-four hours, comfort and convenience supersede modesty. So it was that she padded into the bar at Glasgow's Òran Mór, our venue for the night, in her pyjamas and slippers, holding a toothbrush in her hand, and ordered breakfast. They refused to serve her, on the grounds that she had all the markings of a vagrant.

'I'm with the poetry tour,' she explained to the manager. Not exactly the kind of reference that evokes immediate understanding. 'The big bus outside? Felix Dennis? We're playing here tonight.'

Several other staffers were consulted, schedules were checked, and indeed recognition and acceptance were finally achieved. She was served. But how exhausting. All she wanted was breakfast and a place to brush her teeth.

The Òran Mór, it turned out, would be one of the most hospitable and interesting venues of the tour. Originally a Presbyterian church built in 1862 out of blond sandstone, in 2002 it went from serving God to serving food, drink and entertainment. Inside are two bars, two restaurants, an event space and a nightclub. And as long as you're with the tour, they'll serve you in your pyjamas.

Felix was initially alarmed when he heard the report of MF's morning adventures. 'A vagrant? What the hell is going on?' Once everything was explained to him, however, the usual grin emerged. He was feeling loose and rested, having stopped off in the Lake District for a coffee and smoke during the helicopter ride up to Glasgow. We were also looking at a very full house, a prospect that always boded well for his overall mood.

'Only one more show after this,' I remarked. 'How do you feel about that?'

'Honestly, I haven't thought a thing,' he said. 'You're just trying to get through it. When you're packed like this every night, what is there to complain about?'

What was there to complain about? The sound, the lack of proper smoking facilities, the long helicopter ride, too quiet an audience, bad back – these were his gold-standard gripes wherever we were. They formed the oddly calming background noise that assured you that the man in your presence really was Felix Dennis, perfectionist and crank, not some hired lookalike from the Royal Shakespeare Company. Had he taken some kind of mood medication? Thankfully, he appeared to be back to his normal self after the first set.

'There's a bloody woman there on the side, and she won't clap because she's holding her glass,' he complained to Mick. 'So I just looked at her and she's going tap-tap-tap with her fingers against her glass. Infuriating!'

Marie-France and I had watched his performance from high altitude, in the mezzanine, which sits right beneath the Òran Mór's great jewel: a celestial-themed ceiling mural designed by the Glasgow artist and writer Alasdair Gray. Resplendent with glowing stars and zodiac signs set in a night sky of cobalt blue, it was one of the largest works of public art in Scotland, the perfect roof for a poetry recital. Although the woman with the glass had moderated her applause, what Felix never saw was Marie-France, 30 feet above him, clapping enthusiastically after every poem. It occurred to me that I had never seen her miss one of Felix's sets.

'I'm impressed, MF. You've heard all these poems a hundred times, and look at what a cheerleader you are.'

'Hey, I have to support my man,' she said.

She never ceased to surprise. After the show she mingled downstairs, and ran into Tim and Lydia, a couple she recognised from a poetry reading Felix had done in San Francisco seven years earlier. The show was legendary. On several occasions, Felix had denounced the venue – One Market Street – as the worst ever. He claimed that the reading had taken place in a mall, an acoustical black hole 'where I passed my own echoes as we left at the end of the night.' The show had taken place back in the days when not only the wine was free, but also admission.

'He's correct about it being the worst venue,' said Tim, who was living in SF at the time. 'But it wasn't a mall. It was a luxury atrium in a restaurant. Eighty per cent of the people had no idea who the fuck Felix Dennis was.'

'How was the audience?'

'Exactly the same as this one, except they were younger, and they got drunker. I swear to you, man, it was like a fucking orgy. All these people getting really drunk and feisty and randy. Girls were passing numbers to my wife. They closed the toilets because it was just a sea of vomit. By the time people sat down, it was a mess. Nobody knew what they were appreciating.'

Clearly, I had signed up for the wrong tour.

Last Supper

I once shared a cell with Mandela,
(Would you care for a leg or the rump?)
You'll remember that Maxwell feller?
It was me who convinced him to jump.

I spent a whole year as a hermit
In a trance in a cave in Ubud,
The llama himself will confirm it,
I was praying as hard as I could.

My climb up the face of the Eiger
Is a record, I think, that still stands.
I've spat in the eye of a tyger
As I finished him off with my hands.

I tutored Bruce Lee in ju-jitsu,
And invented the catamaran;
It's only much later it hits you
When you're living as hard as you can.

As for that bloody fool Geller,
He couldn't play poker for squat;
Though he knotted my Parker propeller,
    I took every spoon that he'd got.

You may think Madonna's a lulu,
But I'm telling you now, man to man,
When your dick's being gripped by a Zulu,
You'll be coming as hard as you can.

(The corkscrew's behind you, young feller),
This Petrus is all that I've got,
We're making a dent in the cellar,
But I'm damned if I'll leave it to rot.

They tell me I'm riddled with cancer,
So I'm planning to croak with élan,
If you'll pass the cigars and decanter
I'll be dying as hard as I can.

Felix, never one for long goodbyes, warmly bade us all farewell, then sauntered out of the signing hall, still singing. As he made his way out, the rest of us clapped and cheered – for him, for ourselves and for each other.

For a moment, I thought about running after him and trying, one last time, to get him to tell me exactly who he had pushed off a cliff. Most people doubt the truth of that old story, but I don't. Except for marriage and kids and the quiet life, by then it seemed to me that he was capable of anything, and he wouldn't be the first poet with the blood of vengeance on his hands. It would have made for a great cliffhanger: the whisper in the ear, then the inevitable question of whether or not I'd keep the secret.

For weeks, we had all talked big about the tour after-party. A feast was a must, along with a VIP room, dancing, mayhem and all requisite bacchanalia. The only problem was that our plans had never included an extra body on the bus who actually had the time and energy to organise such an event. Certain that such a person would eventually appear if we drank enough, we retired to the lobby bar of our hotel, the Radisson Blu. At a sprawling round table, we ordered a round with shots and waited for the royal reception to begin.

We had been moving at such a relentless pace for the last week that it seemed impossible to believe it was over. Jack and Jonathan, ever on the prowl, ran out to see if they could scout a better place on a rainy Thursday night in Edinburgh. They returned luckless within half an hour, as we knew they would. It was a noble effort, but there was no point in going elsewhere. All that mattered was that we were all there.

'I have a gift for you,' Wendy said after we sat down. She reached into her bag and pulled out a multicoloured lollipop in the shape of a penis. 'I bought this in Brighton, because you were such a dick about getting food that night in London.'

'You should have given it to me,' I told her. 'I deserved it. I'm going to save it as a reminder not to act like a dick.'

London had been a century ago, in tour time. As the shots kept coming, our voices grew louder and the stuffy barman gave us sidelong glances. He was an idiot because, except for us, the bar was a morgue. Soon Lloyd joined us, then the Class Act boys. We greeted them like they were freed hostages and shouted for more drinks. Not one of us ordered wine.

It got ugly. Caroline accidentally scratched MF in the face, voices began to slur and everyone demanded the presence of Scott and Jerina, who were still in the hospital. When they finally arrived, uproar ensued. Scott's foot, it turned out, was not broken, which gave cause for new rounds.

Towards the end of the evening, they kicked us out of the bar, so we moved to a lounge area and ordered more drinks from room service. Jonathan brought out his laptop and, with a grave look, informed me that there was something he wanted to show me.

'You must promise not to tell Felix about this,' he said.

'Okay, I promise.'

He loaded up a QuickTime movie. The opening credit read 'Das Boot Productions' and I instantly recognised the music that accompanies Felix's poem 'I Made a Garden', before another credit informed me that the title of this presentation was 'I Did Jäger Bombs in a Garden'. The film started out as the same placid visual presentation that he had created for Felix's recital of that poem; there were images of sunrise over Dorsington, trees and flowers, and then Felix's sculpture garden. Then suddenly there was Tom Rooke, leaning forward to kiss the statue of Rosalind Franklin on the lips. He had positioned himself so perfectly that the statue came alive – she seemed to be kissing him back.

'It gets better,' Jonathan said.

A few frames later there was Jack Hardy, stretching to beat Roger Bannister to the finishing tape. More hilarious compositions followed: William Blake poking Tom in the eye, Jack about to bitch-slap Stephen Hawking, Tom resting in Mark Twain's lap like a post-coital lover, then later receiving a kick in the face from Bruce Lee and dutifully lighting a cigar for Isambard Kingdom Brunel. In every photo Jonathan had captured them in perfect position, unlocking an entirely new dimension to Felix's sculpture garden.

Most of the poses were playful and innocent, but since humour was the goal the only thing to do was go all the way. One of the best-loved arrangements in the garden, 'The People Before People', features a group of Neanderthals spear-hunting a woolly mammoth. It seems that one of their spears had lodged itself in Tom Rooke's behind, and going by the expression on Tom's face it was not an unpleasant experience. The transformation from Heroes and Villains to Hilarity and Vulgarity culminated with Jack sodomising Loren Eiseley, who rests on his elbows and knees as he studies a fox. The video ended with a sunset and the words, 'Well done everyone! Now get pissed! It's in your contract.'

'This is brilliant!' I told Jonathan. 'My God, Felix will love this. He'll show it to everyone. Why are you afraid to show it to him?'

Jonathan explained that he had been saving the video for the right time, ideally a celebratory event where it's good-natured intentions would be clear.

'Can you imagine what would happen if it somehow got out before he saw it properly?' Jonathan said. 'If he saw it around the office, or – God forbid – on the Internet? He might blow a gasket.'

This was true. He'd spent millions on his garden – and his poetry presentations. In one fell swoop Jonathan had satirised both. Only with the most persistent badgering was I able to get him to let me write about it, and if this is all the world ever gets to know about 'I Did Jäger Bombs in a Garden', then we shall know what Felix's reaction was. Knowing Felix, however, I won't be surprised if it becomes a major attraction at his garden parties, if not an iPad app that you will be able to download for fifty pence a pop.

In real life there is rarely a poignant ending to a tour, not even a poetry tour. It just ended in a haze. I've played back my recordings from that night a dozen times, and I can't understand a word that was said. We were too loud. The best I can do is to tell how it ended for me, the following morning, with a knock on the door of my hotel room.

It was Jonathan, waking me up as promised for the final group photo. I had slept maybe three hours.

Outside, rain was falling – fine Scottish weather, as they say. I threw on some clothes and ran across the street to the bus. Conveniently, Captain Danger had parked right in front of a café. A lone waiter was in there. He sounded Russian, and looked at me like I was a maniac about to rob him. I held up a fiver.

'This may sound weird, but I need you to take a photograph of a large group of people in front of that bus outside,' I told him. 'It's extremely important. You see, we've all been on tour, and this will be the one group photo. Will you do this?'

Too much information and desperation. He looked at me warily.

'You buy coffee?'

'Certainly. Yes, sure, absolutely.'

'Okay.'

We were freezing and hungover and half asleep. Nobody wanted to have that photo taken, but they did it for me. It all happened so fast afterwards – the goodbyes, the hugs and kisses, the obligatory insults traded with the boys. I wasn't going with them back to London. I would stay a few days and get to know my Scottish family.

Yet they had become family too. Part of me wanted to be with them when Das Boot's door shut and the engine fired to life. This is what happens when you enlist on a Felix Dennis Did I Mention the Free Wine? Poetry Tour. There will almost certainly be more tours, but never another one like this. Felix, of course, wasn't there, but it was his mad and unrepentant vision, his energy and his poetry that had brought us together. The Lone Wolf was always watching.

The bus began to move. I watched, fighting back tears, as it trundled down the Royal Mile and disappeared into the rain.

Edinburgh Guest Poet - Christopher Rush

Poetry is the most private of all languages. Speaking of Shakespeare's Sonnets, Wordsworth said: 'With this key Shakespeare unlocked his heart.' And the sonnets do offer us a rare insight into the heart and soul of a writer whose mind we already know very well from his plays, those masterly expressions of dramatic, impersonalised emotion.

One way of combining personal and impersonal in poetry is to write a dramatic monologue. The soliloquies in Shakespeare's plays are, technically, dramatic monologues, and marvellous examples of the form have been written by Tennyson, Browning and T.S. Eliot.

I can't compete with these guys. But when I was a student in Aberdeen in the 1960s, I amused myself by writing dramatic monologues which I imagined coming out of the mouths and minds of our various lecturers and professors. My own personal favourite however is one I wrote about the old battle-axe who was my landlady in our fresher's year, and this is what I'd like to read you now.

I'd just like to say that this piece began life as a dramatic monologue. Then, when I was writing a satirical novel about education called 'Last Lesson of the Afternoon', I used some of my student memories, disguised the poem as prose, and popped it into a chapter of the novel. Now I'm taking it back out again. But to get it started for you I'll read the few sentences of prose introduction, and your own ear will tell you when the thing has modulated into verse.

One more word of explanation here for any younger members of the audience who will not have experienced landladies of the old Presbyterian school, who hung their houses with large printed notices in every room, informing you what you could or couldn't do there – including the bathroom. There were six of us in those digs: six young male first year students – and one female, who was kept away from us at all times. She had her meals with the landlady and used her bathroom. The notices were clearly intended for us. These were the house rules.

And this is the simple hook on which I hung the poem. Again your ear and your intelligence will tell you when my poetic licence has taken me beyond the actual physical notices into all those implied notices written in invisible letters all over the house – in other words the vibes she gave out, and what she obviously thought of us.

It was a granite grey Victorian terraced house, run by the Ancient of Days, Miss Evans, whose white hair hovered about her head like the frozen white flame of eternity. She'd had a Highland mother but had been sired by a Welsh Baptist, and in her blackest rages the twang shot up and down the accentual scale between Scrabster and Cardiff like Franz Liszt changing keys in the Hungarian Rhapsodies so that when she spoke the word 'whanger', which was what she called the carving knife, it took on a twang which generated its own sexual electricity, as when she referred to her girlhood holidays in Wick, glaring at us as she said it, as if daring us to laugh.

Miss Evans had hung her dwelling with formidable notices made out in large black aggressive letters.

Please close vestibule door quietly.
Do not forget your key.
Main front door will be snibbed and chained
and Chubb-locked in any case by eleven pm,
so be back by eleven or sleep on the streets –
not outside my house, if you please.
Any breakages must be paid for – in advance.
Silence must be observed in the morgue – er, morning room.
Breakfast at 7.30 sharp, on the last stroke of the gong,
which is tuned to Middle 'C', or it's hungry you'll go,
and the same at half past six, be back for dinner
if you please to lend an ear –
that blast forlorn, that gong-tormented 'C'.
And don't stack your books against the wallpaper,
which will mark it and start up a pattern –
no frivolous designs on my kitchen towels –
for it's plain living and high thinking for you, my lads,
you've left Liberty Hall behind you now,
so no bloody liberties here!
Do not smoke in your bedrooms,
drop your filthy sodden fag-ends down the pan,
leave your soapy bristles in the sink,
forget to lift the seat when micturating,
or use more than two squares of tracing paper per visit –
and get your aim straight, will you?
Furthermore, don't dare to come back here
boozed out of your minds
to piss your student grants up against the wall
and darken these respectable premises with your drunken goings-on.
Above all else, top of the list – and you'd better follow this one, loons –
forget whatever plans you've made

for four years fucking at my expense,
for you'll not be dipping your dirty wicks under this roof,
Wick woman or no, turning me into a brothel
while I'm still rattling my chains of asthma
up and down them stairs each night, no –
none of your sodomies and floosies
and fancy women in this establishment
so long as I'm on the prowl, let me tell you,
especially having your ends away with your student nurses
and radiographers and fresh young tarts
who just canna wait to be pulling their knickers down,
the first-class whores that they are,
to let you have your wicked ways with them,
undoing all the good their mothers did
by getting themselves undone before freshers' week's
even one day old - Oh, Jesus Saviour, pilot me! –
and to think of all the salt water that went over
their fathers' heads, these fine old fishermen,
to send them here, scrimping and saving
and shooting and hauling and grafting and dying,
only for them to be shafted by the first spotty bastard
in a brand new scarf
to sneak them back here when my back is turned –
no, it's not on, me buckos,
for I'm a godfearing woman, as the samplers will tell you,
terrible as an army with banners, and I'm not mocked,
immaculate in my life as sacramental linen,
untouched by man and private as the Sphinx,
never let any vile penis enter my front room,
like some I could mention, as near as next door,
keeps to their back and lets out their fore-rooms,

CLOCKWISE FROM TOP LEFT: Felix meets a young fan who produced a photo of Felix from the 60s in Dublin · Jason Kersten sampling the Cork nightlife · 'Yes, it's lovely, really!' Wendy Kasabian and Caroline Rush sample some Guinness

CLOCKWISE FROM TOP LEFT: Dublin audience members enjoying the free wine · Thom Stretton and Caroline Rush after the Dublin show
· More happy audience members at The Button Factory, Dublin · The crew quench their thirst in Dublin
· Stage set-up at The Shaw Theatre, London – note crew members crawling over stage matting

CLOCKWISE FROM TOP LEFT: Setting up at the Contemporary Urban Centre, Liverpool
· The Class Act crew crash out on the ferry home from Dublin

CLOCKWISE FROM TOP LEFT: Felix and his old school chum, Peter Quesnel at Warwick · Jason meets a fan
· Felix meets Mark Frith and his drawing of the Great Oak of Nibley Green

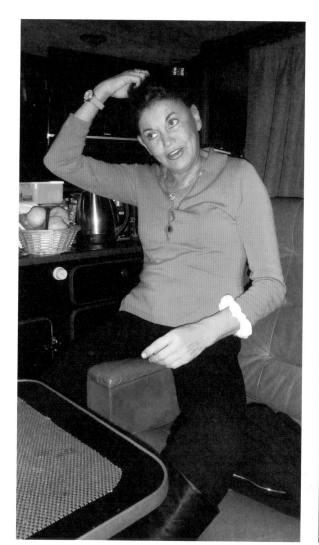

CLOCKWISE FROM TOP LEFT: Marie-France – 'impeccable good humour and yes, savoir-faire'
· Marie-France at the Oran Mor in Glasgow – 'Hey, I have to support my man' · The Crew – 'freezing, hungover and half asleep' in Edinburgh

CLOCKWISE FROM TOP LEFT: Thom Stretton orchestrating the visuals during the show
· Felix's chauffeur, Lloyd Warren, on a rare night off from driving · The Glasgow audience definitely enjoyed the free wine!
· Scottish Poet, Christopher Rush, enthrals the audience at The Hub, Edinburgh

CLOCKWISE FROM TOP LEFT: Felix wrapping the thank you gifts for the crew in Edinburgh · Another busy night of book sales in Edinburgh · The tour bus girls in their matching PJs – Jerina, Caroline, Wendy & Marie-France